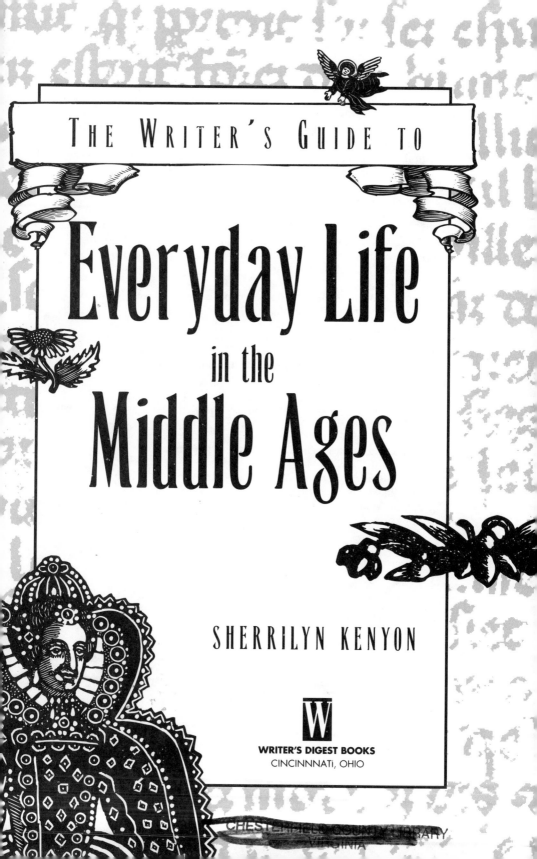

The Writer's Guide to

Everyday Life
in the
Middle Ages

SHERRILYN KENYON

WRITER'S DIGEST BOOKS
CINCINNNATi, OHIO

This hardcover edition of **The Writer's Guide to Everyday Life in the Middle Ages** features a "self-jacket" that eliminates the need for a separate dust jacket. It provides sturdy protection for your book while it saves paper, trees and energy.

Other fine Writer's Digest Books are available from your local bookstore or direct from the publisher.

99 98 97 96   5 4 3 2

Library of Congress Cataloging-in-Publication Data

Kenyon, Sherrilyn
    The writer's guide to everyday life in the Middle Ages / Sherrilyn Kenyon—1st ed.
      p.   cm.
    Includes bibliographical references and index.
    ISBN 0-89879-663-6
    1. Historical fiction—Authorship—Handbooks, manuals, etc. 2. Middle Ages—Historiography—Handbooks, manuals, etc. 3. Civilization, Medieval—Handbooks, manuals, etc. 4. Authorship—Handbooks, manuals, etc. I. Title. II. Title: Everyday life in the Middle Ages.
PN3377.5.H57K46   1995
909.07—dc20
                                  94-43915
                                      CIP
                                      AC

Edited by Jack Heffron
Designed by Sandy Conopeotis
Cover Design by Sandy Conopeotis

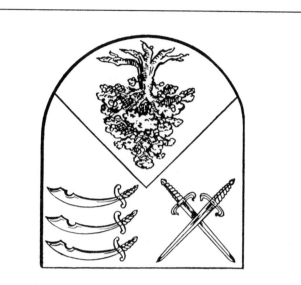

DEDICATION

In memory of Dr. James W. Alexander, who always had time for an eager student's questions. His warm encouragement and insightful comments are sorely missed.

For my mother, who placed that silly suit of armor in the den and captured a young girl's imagination.

My father, who was my first knight in shining armor.

My brother, Steve, who has always been my own special court jester.

My sister, Cathe, who read me *Robin Hood* until she was nearly mad.

And for Ken, who has been my sounding board and devil's advocate these last few years, and who has never allowed me to get away with an unfounded conclusion. Thank you.

ACKNOWLEDGMENTS

DR. VICTORIA CHANDLER, who introduced me to the Haskins Society and who has answered and directed me too many times to count.

DR. TRACY FESSENDEN, who read over sections of the manuscript and made suggestions.

DR. JUDITH KRABBE, who graciously donated her medieval bibliography and whose intelligence, encouragement and smile always inspire me. You are a true role model!

Ms. HARMON at Millsaps College Library, who was so kind and prompt at getting the resources I needed.

RICKEY MALLORY, who assisted with the illustrations and without whom I would have lost my mind.

KIM HENSON JONES and the pictures she graciously donated. *Je t'aime, ma soeur.*

TANYA ANNE CROSBY, whose invaluable insight and suggestions were worth their weight in platinum.

MY HUSBAND, KEN, who never shuddered at the money I spent on research materials and books.

TO THE MEMBERS OF THE SCA and all the years of fun, experience and education they have provided. *May Goddes love blest ye alle!*

AND TO ALL THE MEDIEVAL HISTORIANS AND GRAD STUDENTS I have conversed with on various internet topics who have challenged me, expanded my conclusions, and forced me to defend my positions.

Special Acknowledgments

John Struchen and the entire staff and participants of the Georgia Renaissance Festival, who allowed pictures of their annual event in Fairburn, Georgia. Anyone interested in more information can contact them at: Georgia Renaissance Festival, P.O. Box 986, Fairburn, GA 30213

And to Pat Alderson, Terry Moss and Hank Reinhardt of Museum Replicas Ltd., who graciously donated photographs from their weaponry catalog that specializes in authentic replicas of medieval and renaissance costumes and weapons. For more information: Museum Replicas, P.O. Box 840, Conyers, GA 30207, (404)922-3700

ABOUT THE AUTHOR

Sherrilyn Kenyon has taught a number of classes and workshops in medieval history and writing. Her love of things medieval began at age five when her sister read Howard Pyle's *The Merry Adventures of Robin Hood* to her. At age sixteen, she joined the Society for Creative Anachronism to which she still belongs.

While an undergraduate at the University of Georgia, she became a member of the Charles Homer Haskins Society for medieval historians. She is also a member of the Archaeological Institute of America and an assisting editor for *The Medieval Chronicle*.

Her past works include: *Writer's Digest Character Naming Sourcebook*, and the novels, *Paradise City* and *Daemon's Angel*.

PART THREE:

GOD & WAR

PART FOUR:

PEOPLE & PLACES

INTRODUCTION

Madame, that throgh your newfangelnesse
Many a servaunt have put out of your grace,
I take my leve of your unstedfastnesse
For wel I woot, while ye have lyves space,
Ye kan not love ful half yere in a place;
To newe thing your lust is ay so kene;
Instede of blew, ye may wel were al grene.

So wrote Geoffrey Chaucer in his poem "Against Women Unconstant." Middle English is a fascinating language. When you first hear it, it sounds remarkably foreign. Indeed, I could just as easily be quoting:

Une aventure vus dirai
Dunt li Bretun firent un lai.
Laustic ad nun, ceo m'est vis,
Si l'apelent en lur païs;
Ceo est russignol en franceis
E nihtegale en dreit engleis

Which is Marie de France's twelfth century French Lai *Laüstic*. In hearing the languages, you'll notice they have a great deal in common. After all, with the Norman invasion of 1066, the Germanic Old English was altered forever. Yet even the Medieval French has some holdovers from its Germanic roots. Note the umlauts in the excerpt from *Laüstic*.

Both languages are a bridge from their original roots to the ones we know today. This is one reason why Middle English fascinates me so. After all, it links modern English and Old English.

Littered throughout Middle English, we find Germanic pronunciations and spellings. And littered in modern English, we find a number of Old English words that survive intact with only a slight pronunciation difference: cwene (queen), cyng (king), lust, ken, wisdom, templ (temple) and lytel (little).

So why this focus on language? After all, no one will be writing a book in Old English, Middle English or Medieval French.

Simple. At first glance, the past, much like the above languages, looks complicated, almost unintelligible. Yet if you look at it in pieces as opposed to the whole, what you find are things we do know, things we do understand such as the Old English words above.

Richard Barber in *Henry Plantagenet* wrote that:

> Eight centuries separate us from the age of Henry II.
> With each year's passing our links with the Plantagenet's
> times grow fewer and more slender, and the obstacles to
> understanding the thoughts and ways of a man living in
> his circumstances becomes correspondingly greater.

Where there are historians who concur, I am of the opposing school. True, eight centuries do separate us, but eight hundred years on an evolutionary scale amounts to a microsecond on a twenty-four hour clock—an amount of time so infinitesimal as to be ridiculous.

Just as we can look back on the language and recognize it, so too can we not only understand, but sympathize with Henry II and his situation. We all know what it's like to have something valuable taken from us. Those who run corporations or small businesses, or farmers who have had others take what they've built, know exactly what it's like to lose important property. Though the above is not a kingdom, we can still understand Henry's driving need to retake his promised lands from Stephen.

And the events of his later life are just as understandable. Most parents can relate to having children rebel against them. This happens every day, especially in cases of powerful or rich families where the children are eager for their inheritance.

Or what about Eleanor siding with her children against Henry? Again, this is not unusual. So wherein lies this mysterious element that prevents us from understanding Henry's circumstances and thoughts?

Just like us, he was a human being; he lived, he fought, he struggled, he died.

It is what I term the fallacy of the human ego that makes us look to the past and proudly proclaim our superiority. Have we truly changed so much? Is there a shred of truth to the thought that no other past generation traveled the ground we travel now?

No. In fact, this argument is the same one voiced by teenagers who refuse to believe their parents ever had a youth, ever faced peer pressure or being stood up.

By reading the literature and letters of the medieval period, a researcher is quickly struck by parallels. Let's examine for a moment two twelfth century letters translated by Catherine Moriarity:

To their dear and respected parents M. Marte, knight

2

and M. his wife, M. and S., their sons, send greetings and filian obedience.

This is to inform you that, by divine mercy, we are living in good health in the city of Orleans and are devoting ourselves wholly to study, mindful of the words of Cato, 'To know anything is praiseworthy,' etc. We occupy a good and comely dwelling, next door but one to the schools and market place, so that we can go to school every day without wetting our feet. We have also good companions in the house with us, well advanced with their studies and of excellent habits — an advantage which we well appreciate, for as the Psalmist says, 'With an upright man, thou wilt show thyself upright' etc. Wherefore lest production cease from lack of material, we beg your paternity to send us by the bearer, B., money for buying parchment, ink, desk, and the other things which we need, in sufficient amount that we may suffer no want on your account (God Forbid!) but finish our studies and return home with honour. The bearer will also take charge of the shoes and stockings which you have to send us, and any news as well.

I know my father relates to that letter. Instead of quoting Psalms, I used terms like Pseudo-Isodorian Decretels and quoted Plato to show him his money wasn't being wasted. Indeed, I think any student or parent can relate to the old, "But Mom, Dad, everyone else has a new notebook! How can I keep up with them if all I have is my ratty one from last year?"

And like most parents who lose patience with their children who seem to idle a bit, here's another letter. This one is from Besancon to his son:

It is written, 'He also that is slothful in his work is brother to him that is a great waster.' I have recently discovered that you loved dissolutely and slothfully, preferring license to restraint and play to work and strumming the guitar while the others are at their studies, whence it happens that you have read but one volume of law while your more industrious companions have read several. Wherefore I have decided to exhort you herewith to repent utterly of your dissolute and careless ways that you

may no longer be called a waster and that your shame
may be turned to good repute.

Again, I think most people can relate to this message!

So how is it that myths and misconceptions get started? Why do
people often say, "Oh, how medieval!" as if that is the most backwards thing anything can be?

Well, there is a lot of history that does separate us from the Middle
Ages, and sometimes it's easy to throw all history into one category
and to draw generalizations where generalizations should not be
drawn. If we in our modern twentieth century had to fight for wom-
en's rights, then it is only natural that we are the first to have them.

Actually, women of the past had far more authority than most
women today. For example, can an average woman today hold a
legal court and expect her sentence to be carried out? Can an average woman lead an army? Can an average woman hire or fire her
children's teachers? Of course not. Yet these are typical duties expected of noblewomen, and in certain cases, middle-class women, in
the medieval period.

But what of the laws and church writings that said women had to
subjugate themselves to their husbands? Let's take a moment to look
at our own laws. How many of us pay attention to jay-walking ordi-
nances? Speeding laws? And even with the stiff penalties against driving while intoxicated, how many people every day drive under the
influence of some drug? Medieval people were no different. Some
obeyed the laws, some didn't, and some didn't even know what the
laws were. An example of this comes from Patricia Orr's research on
the years 1194 to 1232. She came across a reference that says no
woman could bring a case to a royal court unless it involved personal
injury to herself or the death of her husband. Yet only three cases
were ever dismissed on these grounds, while literally hundreds of
others were heard regarding everything from theft to murder.

Where it is true that we will never know the exact truth of how
women were treated, I think we can draw a close parallel with our
own society. Some women were loved and treasured and some were
horribly abused. And just as some were abused, others were abusers.
There are a number of cases of women who neglected and abused
their husbands and children.

And though there were laws granting the husband the right to
punish his wife, he was never supposed to hit her in anger or while
drinking. As disturbing as this law may be to some, I hasten to re-

mind everyone that this view can still be found in modern society. In fact, I heard a female caller not long ago on a local talk show say that she thought a husband had a right to punish his wife if the wife deserved it, and this caller was in her twenties.

So why are there so many discrepancies out there? Why do we pick up J.W. Thompson's *Economic and Social History of the Middle Ages* and read that no woman was ever a peddler in the Middle Ages? Then we pick up Maryanne Kowaleski and Judith M. Bennett's article, "Crafts, Gilds, and Women in the Middle Ages: Fifty Years After Marian K. Dale," which says there were a number of women who peddled for a living?

One reason can be found in the dates. Thompson's book is from 1952, whereas Kowaleski and Bennett's article was written in 1989. In thirty years, a lot of important research has been done. New documents and archaeological finds have completely rewritten certain historical beliefs.

In 1961 when Sidney Painter died, his lifelong dream had been to research and write on medieval marriage, a much neglected subject in those days. A few years after that, Georges Duby took the torch and produced two books and a number of articles on the subject. Today we have a larger number of books, papers and articles to draw from.

For this reason, I strongly advise researchers to focus on newer books. True, there is a great deal of value to be found in older works such as those by G.C. Coulton, F.W. Maitland, Henri Pirenne and others. But older books also contain outdated research and thoughts such as Henri Pirenne's statement that the Germanic hordes did not destroy the Roman Empire that "they barbarized it, but they did not consciously germanize it." Though there is some truth to this, the bulk of the sentiment has long since been cast aside. Most modern historians are quick to point out that the hordes had no interest in preserving Roman tradition. Instead they wanted to partake of the riches and advantages of being citizens, but they wanted their own language and laws.

So where does this leave a modern writer, someone who doesn't have time to read every book written on the Middle Ages? Actually, the discrepancies and opposing arguments offer a writer great fodder for a story. Take for a moment Karen Armstrong's theory that the Children's Crusade wasn't a group of children who left for the Holy Land where they either died or were sold into slavery, but was in fact a group of peasants who protested in the countryside for one summer. Depending on which theory a writer uses, there are multiple story line possibilities.

There is nothing easy about the Middle Ages. It was as complex a time as the years we now live in. Society constantly shifted, as did laws, fashions and beliefs. Indeed, many things we now take for granted were formed in the medieval period: purgatory (thirteenth century), marriage as a sacrament (twelfth century), surnames (developed all throughout the period), universities (tenth century), hospitals and more. Even ninety percent of all the classical writings that survive today come down to us only through medieval manuscript copies.

For this reason, I urge all writers to be careful of what old beliefs about the Middle Ages they hold. Just like old wives' tales, these commonly held beliefs can be misleading or incorrect. Only careful research will prevent embarrassing mistakes.

This book is designed as a mere starting point or as a reference to look up much needed information as quickly as possible. Each section offers a brief overview of the subject and should be treated only as such.

Though I have tried to be as thorough as possible and to present facts objectively, I realize that at times I have inserted my own views drawn from my own research. And as with all historical works, time and space prevented me from exploring all angles and arguments.

I would also like to note that though I've had professors and colleagues review my work and have followed some of their guidance, ultimately I had to make the decision on what to include and on what view I hold on certain issues. This book is a reflection of my research, not theirs.

I wish all writers much success with their historical endeavors, and I hope this book provides the reading lists and necessary information to make those books as accurate as possible.

... la chualeo ...
... toic our. biame fairir.
a uefin er apirellie fe li ...
moi fir. chr. er il li fift er,
zoir au fiegr pillens. oe le
... er beue le oiar oont il ci
... u vnir fire ... fe ...
... deur a eft ... f ...
no rgur ... le ...
ucc le noma f. ...
onr. Sur. chr. afer ue ...
fir. ... le fir cor ...
apr ome ...
er. ana fer ce ... n ...
lua moi. ... a a ...

PART ONE

Everyday Life

CHAPTER ONE

FOOD

Food in a castle was served in the great hall, a large room usually on an upper floor. The lord's table was set up along one wall on a small dias, the rest of the tables were positioned in a perpendicular fashion to the lord's dias. Lower tables were called trestle tables, and when the meals were not being eaten, these tables were taken down and stacked in designated areas. The lord, his guests and family who all sat at the lord's table were the only ones to have chairs; everyone else sat on a bench.

Breakfast was a small snack usually served after morning mass. It consisted of a hunk of bread and ale or cider for the retainers and servants. The lord, his family and guests might be served white bread with a cold slice of meat, cheese and wine.

Dinner, served between 10:00 A.M. and noon, was the main meal of the day. A trumpeter or crier would announce the meal at a castle. When a guest entered, the ladies would curtsey and take their seats. The lord might give the guest a light, quick kiss before showing the guest to his seat at the lord's table.

Attendants or pages would bring a washbowl forward and pour water for the guest and lord out of an aquanmanile (an elaborate pitcher). The rest of the diners would wash their hands in a lavabo-type dispenser in the great hall and dry their hands on a long towel. They would then take their seats at the lower trestle tables on benches that often served as their beds at night.

The diners were served in order: first the visiting clergy, the visiting nobles, the lord and his family, then the retainers.

Table settings included a silver salt cellar, a nef and cups. The cups were made of silver, pewter, wood or horn, though the wealthy could have cups made of coconut shells, ostrich eggs, agate or gourds. Spoons were provided, but guests were expected to bring their own knives to table (forks did not appear until the late fourteenth century and weren't commonly used until the Renaissance).

Either wooden bowls were set out with a thick slice, or chunk, of bread lining the bottom, or round bread would be scooped out to form a bowl. The lord and his guests usually had a silver platter and the rest of the diners were served from wooden platters (one platter was shared by two people). From these platters, the food was placed upon a trencher to be eaten. Platters were used solely for serving.

A large trencher made of bread was set on the table (one for every two people). One person sliced the trencher and kept half, and the other person used the second half as a plate. Plates are not found in England until the very end of the fourteenth century.

Dinner began with a blessing from the chaplain followed by a procession led from the unoccupied side of the lord's table by the steward who oversaw the staff. Next came the pantler who distributed bread and butter, the butler and his assistants who poured the wine, beer or ale, and the kitchen assistants who brought in the rest of the first course. A course was cleared completely from the tables before the next was brought in.

Food was either carried up from a lower level of the castle, or brought in from a separate building. As a result, the food was seldom, if ever, more than lukewarm.

Everyday dinners had two or three courses each, and the last course usually consisted of fruits, cheeses, nuts, wafers and spiced wine. A feast could consist of a number of courses and stagger the average person's imagination with the complexity and variety of dishes.

Pages, or cup bearers, made certain no one's cup went empty. When meat was brought into the great hall on a spit, a young gentleman carver would slice it. But since most meat was boiled, a lord or guest would indicate which meats he wanted and a servant or page would place it on his platter. From there, meat was cut and distributed between dining partners so that a lower ranking lord would serve a higher ranking lord, a man would serve a woman, and a young person would serve an elder.

Food was eaten with the fingers, except for broth, which was sipped, and some stews, which were eaten with spoons.

Before the meat was served, the bread would be broken, or the trencher sliced in half, with each person receiving an equal share.

At the end of the meal, the diners would again wash their hands and return to their duties. The trenchers and bowl liners were gathered by servants and given to the almoner who saw that they were distributed to the poor and needy.

Merchants ate in a similar fashion, but their meals were not as large, or their retainers as many. A tablecloth was draped over each table with one side longer to be used by everyone as a napkin. During a festive occasion with many courses, the tablecloth was changed between each course. Each diner had a knife, spoon and a trencher of day-old bread, which wouldn't absorb all the juices of their food as quickly as fresh-baked bread. Blessings were said by the youngest family member or by a visiting clergyman.

A bowl-shaped trencher.

A peasant's meal was much more humble. An average meal generally consisted of porridge, turnips, dark bread (only the nobility had white bread), and beer or ale. A salad might be added that would consist of parsley, borage, mint, rosemary, thyme, purslayne, garlic or fennel, and a vinegar or verjuice dressing. During hog slaughtering season, peasants would eat pork and bacon, but usually fish was the primary source of meat.

Villagers would eat bread—either rye, barley or wheat—that was occasionally mixed with peas or beans. They also enjoyed oatmeal cakes, porridge, fish, cheese curds, watery ale, mead, cider and metheglin.

Supper at the castle was a light meal served at sunset and usually consisted of one main dish, several small side dishes and cheese. After supper, castle occupants might be entertained by a traveling minstrel, acrobat, contortionist, jongleur or storyteller who performed for their food and were usually given coin as well. If no professional entertainers were present, games might be played, or the lady of the hall or a knight might provide entertainment with a song, instrument or a story.

For the lord or his family who might be absent during a meal, or for someone who came unexpectedly and might need food, bread, cold meat, meat pies, cheese and drink were kept in a livery cupboard located in or near the great hall. Some nobles even had a small livery cupboard in their personal chambers, but this was frowned on by the church as a form of gluttony.

The clergy ate only one meal a day. However, during the summer a light supper was permitted in addition to the midday meal. Each order had its own regulations about what and how much food should be eaten. The Carthusians in Germany, for example, ate vegetable platters. French Cistercian monks ate barley bread, and vetch or millet with boiled roots or nettle leaves. The Benedictines forbade meat except for the sick. On fasting days, oysters, fish and poultry were eaten.

Meals in a monastery were supposed to be eaten in silence even though many clergymen would sign to one another while eating. A lector would stand and read inspirational works during the meal.

⚜ ⚜ ⚜

TYPES OF FOOD

Throughout the period, a variety of foods was eaten by all classes. Some of the foods (due to preservation techniques of salting and applying heavy spices to disguise rotting) would be quite unappealing to the twentieth century palate. Nobility tended to eat mostly meats and pastries. Merchants also consumed a lot of meat, but would also eat vegetables. The poor ate a diet predominately of vegetables and dark breads.

The most common vegetables (which were dubbed commoners' food) were onions, peas, beans, cabbage, parsley, shallots and potherbs. Cucumbers and leeks were avoided since most considered

A flat, sliced trencher that is shared by two people.

them unhealthy. Tomatoes, potatoes and Indian corn did not exist in Europe until the sixteenth century.

Common meats included the following:

Birds: starlings, vultures, gulls, herons, storks, cormorants, swans, cranes, peacocks, capons and chickens.

Seafood: dogfish, porpoises, seals, whale, haddock, cod, salmon, sardines, lamprey, dolphins, tunnies and eels.

Other meats: venison, mutton and pork. Horse meat was forbidden by the church.

Fruits in the Middle Ages were smaller and usually grown in the wild. Raw fruits were thought unwholesome and were seldom served. Fruits mainly consisted of apples, plums, pears, peaches and nuts. Citrus fruits, such as oranges and lemons, were not found in England until the Crusades, and even then they were rare treats. The first recorded large shipment of oranges didn't occur until the late fourteenth century.

Desserts consisted of cheeses, cakes, wafers, spiced wines, cookies, waffles and jellies.

Nobility drank wine, which was sometimes spiced to cover the taste of souring and often diluted or mixed with honey or cinnamon. Mulled wine was the only drink served hot. Lower classes drank mead, ale and beer. The clergy scented their mead with herbs and honey and sometimes added water.

All medieval dishes relied heavily on spices for a number of reasons, the largest being that spices covered the taste of spoiling meat. Garlic was used so heavily by the French that the crusaders offended the people of Constantinople with their breath!

Sugar, one of the most valuable spices, was expensive to import, but from the twelfth century onward, it was a common ingredient in England. Sugars from Alexandria were especially coveted because they were flavored with rose and violets. The most common spices were pepper, mustard, garlic, cloves, vinegar, verjuice, cinnamon, almonds and saffron. Wine and ale were often used to cook fish.

MANNERS

Since the platters and trenchers were shared among the nobility and merchant class, stringent rules of etiquette applied to table manners. People were expected to wash their hands before eating. If dining with the king, a person must bow to the nef before passing it.

People were to always wipe their mouths before taking a drink from the goblet (cups were also shared between two people). Diners ate slowly, taking small bites. They were never to speak with their mouths full, nor were they to take a drink with food still in their mouths. Knives were used for cutting and were not supposed to be placed in the mouth. Spoons were set on the table, not left in the bowl.

Diners were not to gnaw on bones with their teeth, poke their fingers in eggs, spit across the table, wipe their mouths on their sleeves, or bite into the trencher, since this was given to the poor to eat.

Like today, elbows were not supposed to be put on the table, soup was not to be slurped, and there was no belching, leaning over the food, or picking any orifice. No one was supposed to wipe their teeth or knife on the tablecloth, or butter bread with their thumbs.

Food was not to be plunked down in the salt cellar, nor was food to be blown upon to cool it (although, just as people presently do, this often went unheeded). Scraps were not to be fed to the dogs while the diners ate, and many etiquette books spoke against tossing scraps to the dogs even after the meal.

Assorted Food Facts

Food imports and exports played a vital part in trade. England exported fish, cheese and ale and imported raisins, figs, dates, olive oil, wine, almonds, rice and pomegranates. Spain was known for exporting sugar, preserved fruits and syrups. France was known for exporting wine, and Italy for pies.

Food was usually plentiful in the spring and summer, provided there were no droughts, crop failures or pillaging. In winter, cow's milk was scarce and seldom used to cook with.

To ensure survival, meats were salted and stored using one of two methods: dry salting (burying meat in salt) or brine curing (soaking meat in a salt solution). Until the fourteenth century, several types of fish were not gutted before they were preserved.

Due to the heavy amount of meats and pastries consumed by the upper classes, many health problems existed, such as skin irritations, scurvy, tooth decay, heart disease, and numerous infections from bad meat.

For main dishes, cooks paid special attention to the appearance of the food. Swans were cooked fully feathered; heads and other parts of animals were either left on or sewed on after cooking. Many subtleties (sculptures of jelly, sugar and paste) were made.

Common Dishes of Scotland and England

A few common Scottish dishes include:

- Antholl Brose: Made from ale, oatmeal and honey.
- Barley Bannocks: A type of bread made from barley, flour, salt and buttermilk.
- Carrageen Jelly: Made from seaweed and milk.
- Colcannon: A stew made from cabbage, turnips and carrots.
- Crowdie: In the Highlands, it's a type of cheese; in the Lowlands, it's milk and oatmeal.
- Forfar Bridies: A mincemeat pastry.
- Gundy: A type of candy made with sugar, butter and black treacle. Best when seasoned with cinnamon.
- Haggis: A sheep's bladder stuffed with onions, oatmeal, liver, heart and beef.
- Hotch-Potch: A type of stew made with beef or mutton.

Beverages include:

- Pirr

- Blaand
- Heather Ale
- Drammach.

In England some common dishes include:

- Stuffed Pigling—pigling stuffed with nuts, cheese, eggs, spices, bread.
- Entrayale—a dish made of sheep's stomach. The stomach is stuffed with eggs, vegetables, bread, cheese and pork.
- Lampreys in Galytyne—a type of spiced lamprey dish.
- Blackmanger—a chicken dish made with rice, almonds and sugar.
- Mortrews—a meat dish made with eggs and bread crumbs.
- Viaund Royal
- Capon de Haut de Grace
- Venison en Frumenty—venison and whole wheat boiled in milk and heavily spiced.
- Frumenty Pudding—a wheat, milk pudding.
- Leche Lumbarde
- Blaundesorye

Beverages include:

- Cowslip wine
- Dandelion wine
- Elderberry wine
- Apple beer

RECIPES

Water for washing hands: Boil sage, rosemary, bay leaves or chamomile in water. Strain, then cool and pour in a bowl.

Mead: Dissolve four pounds of honey in a gallon of water with half an ounce of ginger. Boil for approximately forty-five minutes, then pour into a barrel or wooden container. Before it cools completely, add yeast and wait for it to ferment. After fermentation, seal and store for six months.

Lampreys in Galytyne: Skin and gut a lamprey, making sure to keep the blood in another container for later use. Roast the lamprey on a spit, and save the grease. Mix ground raisins with rose petals and combine with bread crusts and vinegar, or verjuice. Add powder ginger and the blood and grease to the raisin mixture, then boil together and salt to taste.

Cheese Crowdie: Heat soured milk until it separates. Do not boil. Strain the whey. Season the solid cheese block with salt, pepper and a dab of garlic. Let stand for a day or two.

Haggis: Soak a sheep's bladder in salted water for at least twelve hours. Turn the roughened side out, then wash the small bag. Hang the windpipe over the edge of the pot. Cover with water and boil for an hour or two. Afterwards, cut off the pipe and gristle. Finely chop the heart and half of the liver. Add two chopped onions, garlic and oatmeal, and moisten with broth. Put the mixture inside the large bag and sew closed. Boil for approximately three hours, cutting a small hole when the bag begins to swell.

Eels: Skin and gut eels, then cut into chunks and place them in a pan of salted water. Add chopped parsley, garlic and pepper. Boil until the eel chunks begin to split.

Blackmanger: Cut chicken into chunks, and blend with rice that has been boiled in almond milk and salt and seasoned with sugar. Cook until mixture is very thick and garnish with anise and fried almonds.

FOR FURTHER READING

T. Austin, *Two Fifteenth Century Cookery Books*.
T. Bayard, *A Medieval Home Companion*.
M. Black, *The Medieval Cookbook*.
F.J. Furnivall, *The Babees' Book: Medieval Manners from the Young*.
J. and F. Gies, *Life in a Medieval City*.
J. and F. Gies, *Life in a Medieval Village*.
P.W. Hammond, *Food and Feast in Medieval England*.
D. Hartley, *Food in England*.
U.T. Holmes, Jr., *Daily Living in the Twelfth Century*.

Chapter Two

Clothing

n the early Middle Ages, very little separated the dress of the nobility from that of the peasantry. The styles of clothing and the types of fabric they wore were very much alike. This similarity in dress, however, should not suggest an egalitarian society in which the nobility was uninterested in distinguishing themselves from the common folk. The similarity was due mostly to limited trade caused by poor travel conditions. Remember that the roads at this time were terrible, so merchants and peddlers could not go far with their carts and wagons. And even those roads that were passable were riddled with thieves who often killed travelers to steal their belongings.

Throughout this period, most nobles, in order to set themselves apart, relied on jewels, which were easier to obtain, especially in the North, where mining was prevalent. In the mid to late eleventh century this situation began to change. The roads gradually improved, making it easier for peddlers to move their wares from place to place. Also, the growing strength of the kings and nobles to control their domains lessened the risk of robbery and violence along the roads. This new mobility led to an increase in trade, bringing a greater variety of fabrics and colors and fashions to those who could afford them. These luxuries, of course, were too expensive for the peasants, but the wealthy seized the opportunity and their fashions began to change.

From this time forward, dress denoted stature and wealth, much as it does today. During the late Middle Ages, sumptuary laws were instituted to ensure that certain fabrics and styles were reserved for those who had a right to wear them. Fashion police would actually patrol the streets checking men and women to make sure they were wearing the appropriate clothing.

As you'll see in this chapter, fashions changed throughout the Middle Ages. To provide you with an overview of these changes, I've divided the period into units of roughly fifty to seventy years. You should not, however, conclude that fashions changed more slowly in the Middle Ages than they do today. We simply lack the space in this book to note every change as it occurred.

WOMEN

By studying manuscripts, we can infer that women's fashions did indeed change quickly. Some trends lasted for decades while others came and went in a couple of years. The women's kirtle, for example, changed from being a large, voluminous mass to a laced, form-clinging dress, the neck and sleeves of which were routinely changed. Sleeves often were detachable so that the woman could keep the main, most expensive part of the dress while still remaining fashionable. In fact, in the later Middle Ages, many women's trousseaus consisted of bolts of fabric with only a few gowns because the fashions changed so quickly that any gowns they brought to the marriage would soon be dated.

1066 to 1087

Undergarment: An under-tunic or smock was the only undergarment worn. It was an under-dress only visible when the kirtle's sleeves or hem fell short.

Hose: Gartered at the knee.

Shoes: Leather and rose to just above the ankle.

Dress: Called a kirtle.

Girdles: Long and worn around the hips.

Cloaks: Semi-circular, they were worn long and fastened by cord or brooch.

Hair: Worn long and sometimes plaited, it was covered by a long, finely woven veil that was wound about the neck. At times, a circlet was used to keep it in place.

Fabrics: Nobles wore linen and wool; peasants wore russet.

Colors: Red, green, light blue, gray, yellow, red-brown, brown, black.

1087 to 1154

Undergarment: The sleeves were full and the entire smock was "broom sticked" (twisted while wet and dried so as to achieve a crinkled effect).

Hose: Same as before.

Shoes: Same as before.

Dress: Called a kirtle or gown.

Girdles: Same as before, except at state functions a longer girdle was used. Women wrapped this around their upper waist, then doubled it in back and tied on low on their hips (1125 to 1175).

Cloaks: From the East, a *pelisse* came into fashion. It was a short, coat-like garment that fastened at the waist and hung just below the knee.

Hair: Girls wore their hair loose. After 1120, hair was wrapped in ribbon or cloth and was allowed to hang to the knee or lower. If a woman couldn't grow her hair to the fashionable length, false hair was used. Between 1120 and 1150, the veil was worn loose, down the back and secured to the head with a circlet made of gold, silver or silk.

Fabrics: The weave became finer. Nobles wore silk, linen and wool.

Colors: Red, green, light blue, blue, gray, yellow, red-brown, brown and black.

1154 to 1199

Undergarment: The smock sleeves became tight again and a little longer. If the kirtle was cut short, then the bottom of the smock would be shown.

Hose: Still gartered at the knee.

Shoes: Still cut low and made of leather.

Dress: Called a kirtle or gown.

Girdles: Not as popular during this period.

A basic kirtle. Sleeves varied according to fashion.

Cloaks: Woven with heavier material, they remain the same as before.

Hair: The plaits began to fade from fashion, though they are still found at the turn of the century. Hair was wound about the head. During the reign of Richard, the short veils became popular and were held in place by gold or silken bands. Around 1170, the barbette was introduced (page 27), and ca. 1190 the wimple came into fashion. The wimple was wound about the neck, tucked into the kirtle and was pinned to the hair.

Fabrics: Scarlet was introduced, silks, linen, heavily embroidered cloth, wool. The lower classes wore coarser wool and russet.

Colors: Scarlet, watchet, green, yellow, tawny, red, red-brown, black and gray.

1199 to 1272

Undergarment: Didn't change much, but it was no longer revealed by the nobility.

Hose: Same as before.

Shoes: Same as before.

Dress: Called a kirtle or gown.

Girdles: Leather or silk, though still not worn much at home. Long purses often dangled from them.

Cloaks: Lined with fur and embroidered.

Hair: Hair began being coiled on either side of the head. In 1216, short veils and hats returned and often concealed the hair. Around 1220, the fillet of linen was often worn with the barbette. During trips, women also wore small round hats.

Fabrics: Same as before.

Colors: Purple, scarlet, watchet, red, tawny, yellow, brown, red-brown, green, murrey and gray.

Lower classes: Aprons began to be worn and also a sleeveless super-tunic (1216 to 1272).

1272 to 1307

Undergarment: Same as before.

Hose: Same as before.

Shoes: Had pointed toes.

Dress: Called a kirtle.

Girdles: Seldom worn.

Cloaks: Made full and long, they were still made from heavier materials and lined with fur or a lighter fabric. Buttons began to replace other fasteners.

Hair: Caul and frets began to be worn. They were the thick silk or gold nets that most people associate with the period. Some women still continued to wear their hair coiled around each ear. The wimple persisted along with the shorter veil. Widows wore a pleated wimple that covered their chins. The wimple could also be worn without a veil or hat. The other types of headdresses were also still worn. Young girls and women also wore their hair loose with a silk or gold band.

Fabrics: Velvet (appeared around 1303) was reserved for royalty. Fustian, a silky material that was similar to velvet, appeared around the same time and was used for the lesser nobility. Scarlet, wool and linen were also worn. Serge also appeared at the turn of the century, but was used for outer garments. Russet, canvas and linen were used by the rest.

Colors: Purple, scarlet, murrey, watchet, green, gray, reddish brown, red, light blue, tawny, brown and slate.

1307 to 1327

Undergarment: The smock was now called the kirtle and became a visible, vital part to dressing. Sleeves were still form fitting.

Hose: Same as before.

Shoes: Same as before.

Dress: Called a surcoat.

Cloaks: Same as before, but during the period, coats of arms began to be embroidered on them.

Hair: Veils became more popular. They were either worn with a thin gold or silk band, or were draped over a wider band. The barbette fades during this period and vanishes from fashion.

Fabrics: Taffeta (very expensive), velvet, kersey, scarlet, fustian, linen, wool, russet and canvas.

Colors: Silver and gold appeared but were reserved for royalty. Purple, scarlet, murrey, watchet, green, gray, reddish brown, red, flame, white, light blue, tawny, brown and slate.

1327 to 1377

Undergarment: Now two gowns were worn—the smock and the kirtle. Unmarried women often wore only these two gowns. Buttons, tippets (narrow white bands that flowed from the elbow to ankle), and fitchets (slashes in the kirtle) also came in during this time.

Hose: Same as before.

Shoes: Same as before.

Dress: Called a cote-hardie, and also the sideless surcoat was still worn.

Cloaks: Narrow cloaks fastened with silken cords or brooches began to be worn for state functions. Otherwise, cloaks remained the same.

Hair: Hair was still coiled around the ears and head. Cauls and frets now took on a square shape and were sometimes embroidered. Veils became transparent and very finely woven. Around 1350, a ruffled veil became fashionable.

Fabrics: Silk, satin, velvet, taffeta, scarlet, linen, wool, flannel, russet and canvas.

Colors: Purple, gold, silver, scarlet, murrey, watchet, green, gray, reddish brown, red, light blue, tawny, brown and slate. A reddish orange and a bright tan color came in, but both were expensive.

1377 to 1399

Undergarment: The smock was now also called a chemise. Made from fine linen and silk, it remained unchanged.

Hose: Same as before.

Shoes: Same as before.

Dress: Called a cote-hardie. The surcoat was sideless with the skirt made of a separate material than the bodice. By the end of the reign, women adopted the houppelande. High necked, it was either worn unbelted, or with a high belt that fastened just beneath the breasts.

Cloaks: Same as before.

Hair: Coronets were worn for court or state functions. The square cauls gave way to rounded ones. Chaplets also became fashionable. They were thick, padded, round hats that were embroidered, set with jewels and worn with a veil. During this time, the wimple was relegated to the lower classes.

A cap commonly worn by the poorer classes from 1300 until the end of the Middle Ages.

Fabrics: Silk, freize, satin, velvet, taffeta, scarlet, linen, wool, flannel, russet, canvas and serge.

Colors: Black, purple, scarlet, green, white, gray, red, blue and russet.

1399 to 1413

Undergarment: Same as before.

Hose: Same as before.

Shoes: Same as before.

Dress: The cote-hardie gradually gave way to the houppelande. The front was slit at the neck, and toward the end of the period, a white collar was added that spanned to the shoulders. During this time, the gold and silver S-necklace was worn around the collar of the houppelande.

Belt: Worn just under the breasts.

Cloaks: For state functions they were wide and circular, fastened with silken cords or brooches. It became fashionable to embroider the coats of arms on the back.

A hat with a barbette (around the chin) and crispinette (covering the hair). This hat style was popular among the nobility in the thirteenth century.

Hair: Around 1401, the rolled band became small and flat, and by the end of the period, all headdresses dipped low in the front. Veils were small and worn with other hair dresses. Cauls were still worn, some now protruding out from the side of the head.

Fabrics: Velvet was now used by all nobility. Also worn were silk, freize, satin, brocade, taffeta, scarlet, linen, wool, flannel, russet, canvas and serge.

Colors: Black, purple, scarlet, green, white, gray, red, blue and russet.

1413 to 1422

Undergarment: same as before.

Hose: Same as before.

Shoes: Same as before.

Dress: Called houppelande. The high collar disappeared after 1415, and the collar was laced closed.

Cloaks: The narrow cloak was still used for court and state functions. The full, hooded cloak was used for traveling.

Hair: Headdresses became very wide.

Fabrics: Lawn was introduced around 1415. Still used were velvet, silk, freize, satin, brocade, taffeta, scarlet, linen, wool, flannel, russet, canvas and serge.

Colors: Black, purple, scarlet, green, white, gray, yellow, tawny, bright tan, red, blue and russet.

1422 to 1461

Undergarment: Same as before.

Hose: Same as before.

Shoes: Same as before.

Dress: Long sleeves disappeared. Very high waisted, the gown for court wear formed a sharp V (trimmed with fur or linen) in front and in back.

Cloaks: Full and no longer worn for state functions.

Hair: Heart-shaped headdresses became popular. A wide variety were worn. Hair was plucked or shaved (including eyebrows) so as to disappear beneath the headdress.

Fabrics: Damask was introduced around 1415. Still used were velvet, lawn, silk, freize, satin, brocade, taffeta, scarlet, linen, wool, flannel, russet, canvas and serge.

Colors: Black, purple, scarlet, green, white, gray, yellow, tawny, bright tan, red, blue and russet.

Cosmetics

A variety of cosmetics was used throughout the period. Perfume was made from myrrh, cassia, frankincense, cedar, cypress, sesame, olive and almond. During the Crusades, many men and traders brought new scents to Europe. A perfumer's guild was founded in France in 1190. After this date we see new perfumes including musk, castor and ambergris.

Many women used a white lead base for their complexion, which proved as disastrous to them as it had to Roman women since the lead seeped into the skin and caused madness or painful skin disorders. Chalk, cuttlefish powder, flour, egg whites, camphor, and lard were also used. Rouge ranged from orangish colors to pinks. Eyeshadow was available in gray, brown, green and red. During the thirteenth century, a desire for a natural look led to the development of rose and flesh-colored bases. Eyeliner was also worn, and the lashes could be darkened with soot. Many of these cosmetics were powdered, and women would add saliva or water to apply them.

Hair could be dyed blonde, red, chestnut, black, or brown with a variety of mixtures. Hair was removed with depilatories, razors and tweezers. Curling irons could also be used to curl hair. Hairpins were made from a gamut of substances including ivory, bone, wood, gold, silver and metal.

Jewelry remained popular throughout the period for both sexes. Popular items were rings (some worn above the knuckle), earrings, necklaces and bracelets.

MEN

As a rule, rich men of the Middle Ages were extremely fashion oriented. In fact, King John of England made sure his wedding attire was much more grand and elaborate than that of his second wife, Isabella of Angouleme. Men's fashions changed quickly and often and they, like the women, were regulated during the Later Middle Ages by the sumptuary laws.

Though the long, pointed shoes were indeed fashionable from the latter point of the Early Middle Ages on (the length of the toe, shape and position of the point changed regularly), the curled over, genie-type shoes most people think of for this period were not worn until the last half of the fifteenth century.

1066 to 1087

Shoes: Made of leather, they came up to and fastened around the ankle.

Pants: Called breeches or braies. Drawstring pants had a loose fit and either enclosed the foot or had a stirrup bottom. Colored hose were often pulled up over the pant legs and cross-gartered with strips of cloth.

Shirt: Called a tunic or shirt. Longer shirts were used for state functions.

Cloaks: Either square or circular, they were fastened by brooches or cords.

Hair: Normans wore their hair short with the back of the head shaved. Their faces were clean shaven. Saxons wore longer hair and beards.

Fabrics: Nobles wore linen and wool; peasants wore russet.

Colors: Red, green, light blue, gray, yellow, red-brown, brown and black.

1087 to 1100

Shoes: The cut became more exaggerated.

Pants: Same as before, but more form fitting. Hose were also still worn, but no longer seen except when worn beneath the slit tunic.

Shirt: These became longer, trailing on the ground in some cases. Some were slit to the waist, and all were pulled over the girdle. By the end of the period, fuller sleeves became popular.

Cloak: Longer and fuller for the nobility. Fur-lined cloaks were also popular. The pallium was introduced. It was a shorter cloak that draped across the hips and over the shoulder. Lower classes wore the shorter, less full cloaks.

Hair: Shoulder-length hair became the fashion along with short beards. Head bands were sometimes worn and for bad weather, men would wear a phrygian cap.

Fabrics: Nobles wore linen and wool; peasants wore russet.

Colors: Red, green, light blue, gray, yellow, red-brown, brown and black.

1100 to 1154

Shoes: Toes were long and pointed and they came in a variety of styles, such as boots and cut-away shoes.

Pants: The breeches were the same as before until 1150 when the longer hose caused the breeches to be shortened to the knee. The hose reached past the knee and fastened into the waistband of the breeches.

Shirt: Nobility continued to wear the longer tunics, but around 1150 they were gathered at the sides. The lower classes wore shorter tunics. Both full and tight sleeves were worn.

Hood and gorget. These were popular from 1100 through the middle of the twelfth century.

Cloaks: No significant changes.

Hair: Still rather long with bangs becoming popular. The gorget was introduced—a circular cloth that draped over the shoulders. Also popular was the hood with a pointed back.

Fabrics: Nobles wore linen and wool; peasants wore russet.

Colors: Red, green, light blue, gray, yellow, red-brown, brown and black.

1154 to 1199

Shoes: Longer boots that reached to the calf were popular. Low-cut shoes were also popular. Another innovation was a longer hose with a leather sole. These were cross-gartered and worn without shoes. The poorer classes continued to wear ankle boots.

Pants: Breeches remained the same. Crossbands were worn all the way up the leg. Poorer classes and travelers wore them to the knee.

Shirt: Tunics remained the same until around 1185 when the sleeves began to be cut differently. The wide cuffs gave way to a tight-fitting cuff. The tunic had a bat-wing cut, and a slit was added down the front.

Girdle: More ornate with one long end. Purses also began to be worn dangling from the girdle.

Cloaks: Same as before. Travelers wore skins with hoods.

Hair: Shorter hair became fashionable. Around the turn of the century, small, pointed beards were worn. A variety of hats was worn, including the phrygian, wide-brimmed, flat hats, and smaller hats with upturned brims.

Gloves: Became very popular during this time.

Fabrics: Scarlet was introduced. Still popular were silk, linen, heavily embroidered cloth, and wool. The lower classes wore coarser wool and russet.

Colors: Scarlet, watchet, green, yellow, tawny, red, red-brown, black and gray.

1199 to 1272

Shoes: The toes became more pointed.

Pants: Same as before, but after 1200 crossbands disappeared.

Shirt: The tunic remained the same, but after 1200 a shorter supertunic began to be worn over it. Like the surcoat, the supertunic could be open on the sides, or the sides could be sewn shut. Pelissons were also popular. These were fur-lined supertunics. Another popular supertunic appeared around 1225. This one had pleated shoulders and long, full sleeves, but a slit was cut in the middle of it for the arm to pull through and a hood was attached. Young men wore the shorter tunics.

Girdle: Same as before, but worn over the supertunic.

Cloaks: Used only for state functions and traveling. The small shoulder cape developed dagged edges (deep scallops). Dagged edges appeared also on tunics and supertunics.

Hair: Beards went out of fashion and hair remained above-shoulder length. The coif hat appeared. Unlike the coifs made of mail, these were more like the barbette—a white linen cap that fastened under

A dagged-edged cape. This style was popular through most of the thirteenth century.

the chin. The black coifs were reserved for the elderly or learned. Other hats were worn over either color.

Fabrics: Same as before.

Colors: Purple, scarlet, watchet, red, tawny, yellow, brown, red-brown, green, murrey and gray.

1272 to 1307

Shoes: Same as before, but now they were lined with fur and had embroidered bands around the instep.

Pants: Same as before.

Tunic: Same as before, only minor changes such as a high collar sometimes took the place of the hood on the supertunic. The sleeves were less ornate and many supertunics were lined with fur. Buttons started to replace other fasteners.

Cloaks: Serge cloaks were used for traveling and inclement weather.

Gloves: Remained popular.

Hair: Same as before with the only noted change being the lengthening of the hood into a liripipe, which was often coiled about the head.

Fabrics: Velvet (appeared around 1303) was reserved for royalty, and fustian (a silky material that was similar to velvet that appeared around the same time) was used for the lesser nobility. Scarlet, wool and linen were also worn. Serge also appeared at the turn of the century, but was used for outer garments. Russet, canvas and linen were used by the rest.

Colors: Purple, scarlet, murrey, watchet, green, gray, reddish brown, red, light blue, tawny, brown and slate.

1307 to 1327

Shoes: Same as before.

Pants: Same as before.

Shirt: Same as before except the sleeves were more form fitting. Young men still wore the shorter tunics and usually left their sleeves unbuttoned and hanging free from the elbow. Around 1320, the garnache appeared. It was a wider type of supertunic that fell off the shoulders and to the elbows. The sides could either be open or sewn shut.

Girdles: Only worn by youths or under supertunics.

Cloaks: Same as before.

Hair: Same as before. The caps remained unchanged as well.

Fabrics: Taffeta (very expensive), velvet, kersey, scarlet, fustian, linen, wool, russet and canvas.

Colors: Silver and gold appeared but were reserved for royalty. Purple, scarlet, murrey, watchet, green, gray, reddish brown, red, flame, white, light blue, tawny, brown and slate.

A liripipe coiled and worn about the neck. This style was popular from the middle to the end of the thirteenth century. A liripipe was also worn uncoiled, trailing down the back of the wearer.

1327 to 1377

Shoes: Same as before.

Pants: Same as before until around 1350. From this point on, they attached to the gypon. Long hose with soles were also still worn.

Shirt: The tunic became known as the gypon and the supertunic as the cote-hardie. Both became increasingly shorter and tighter. By 1360, they barely covered the hips. Buttons fastened the front and sleeves. Sleeves were long, covering the knuckles. In the beginning of the period, sleeves were still left unbuttoned and hung from the elbow. This was replaced by the tippet, a long, white streamer that attached to the upper arm. The poorer citizens wore a longer cote-hardie. Elders wore the looser gypons and cote-hardies.

Girdles: Flat, jewelled girdles became popular. Girdles now rested very low on the hips.

Cloaks: Semicircular and richly lined, cloaks fastened on one shoulder with two buttons.

Hair: Same as before. Small beards reappeared. Gorget was sometimes worn singularly. The only hat addition was a beaver hat. Also, hats began to be worn indoors. Around 1350, plumes became popular.

Fabrics: Silk, satin, velvet, taffeta, scarlet, linen, wool, flannel, russet and canvas.

Colors: Purple, gold, silver, scarlet, murrey, watchet, green, gray, reddish brown, red, light blue, tawny, brown and slate. A reddish orange and a bright tan came in, but both were expensive. Men also started wearing parti-colored clothes, which were very popular by the second half of the period.

1377 to 1399

Shoes: By the turn of the century shoes were exceedingly long and the tips were curled back and attached to the leg just below the knee. Pattens or galouches, as they were sometimes called, were worn during inclement weather. Red hose became extremely fashionable. Cod-pieces, which were tiny triangles fastened to the front of the hose by laces and tags, also became fashionable.

Shirt: The gypon was padded in the front and the sleeves were still tight. The cote-hardie was still short, but the collar became high and rolled down. Bagpipe sleeves became popular (the sleeves were very full and gathered into a tight cuff). Around 1380, the houppelande became popular. The high neck was often rolled down and heavily embroidered. The length varied from mid-calf to floor to those that trailed on the ground (for formal occasions). It hung in large folds and the sleeves were full. The skirt was either slit up the sides or down the front. Dagged edges became fashionable. Folly bells were sewn into a circle around the shoulders or onto the girdle. Jeweled collars, fur trim and chains worn around the shoulders were also popular.

Hair: Same as the past until around 1395 when the ends were curled outward and hair became longer. Hats remained popular. Toward the turn of the century, the brims became taller and were rolled over.

Fabrics: Silk, freize, satin, velvet, taffeta, scarlet, linen, wool, flannel, russet, canvas and serge.

Colors: Black, purple, scarlet, green, white, gray, red, blue and russet.

1399 to 1422

Shoes: The long toes fell out of favor. Boots became taller, reaching over the knee for traveling. Around 1410, boots started being laced and/or buckled on the outside to make them fit more snugly to the leg.

Pants: The long hose were still popular.

Shirt: The gypon was still worn but was no longer visible. The cote-hardie's pleats were now sewn into place. The houppelande was mostly the same, but now the collar had a split in the front and shoulder pieces were added to make the wearer's arms appear larger. Dagged edges remained popular.

Hair: The old Norman fashion returned: short hair, often shaved in the back. Hats remained fashionable and chaplets were worn.

Fabrics: Velvet was now worn by all nobility. Silk, freize, satin, brocade, taffeta, scarlet, linen, wool, flannel, russet, canvas and serge.

Colors: Black, purple, scarlet, green, white, gray, red, blue and russet.

1422 to 1461

Shoes: Pointed toes became popular again. Thigh-high boots were also fashionable.

Pants: Same as before.

Shirt: The gypon's collar became higher and now showed. The cote-hardie was the same except for a longer length. The houppelande didn't change much except for the collar, which was now cut low, and the slits on the sides and front, which were no longer seen.

Girdle: Worn very low on hips.

Hair: The Norman fashion was still popular, but around 1455 longer hair became more popular. Hats were still fashionable.

Fabrics: Damask was introduced around 1415. Velvet, lawn, silk, freize, satin, brocade, taffeta, scarlet, linen, wool, flannel, russet, canvas and serge.

Colors: Black, purple, scarlet, green, white, gray, yellow, tawny, bright tan, red, blue and russet.

FOR FURTHER READING

Nancy Bradfield, *Historical Costumes of England 1066 to 1968.*
Iris Brooke, *English Costume of the Later Middle Ages.*
Francois Boucher, *20,000 years of Fashion: The History of Costume and Personal Adornment.*
Theodore Child, *Wimples and Crisping-Pins.*
C.W. Cunningham, *Handbook of English Medieval Costume.*
P. Cunningham and C.W. Cunningham, *A History of Underclothes.*
Joan Evans, *A History of Jewelry 1100 to 1870.*
Dorothy Hartley, *Medieval Costume and Life.*
Carl Kohler, *A History of Costume.*
John Peacock, *Costume 1066 to 1966.*
Aileen Ribeiro, *Dress and Morality.*
C.H. Smith, *Ancient Costumes of Great Britain and Ireland.*

CHAPTER THREE

MEDICINE

edicine in the Middle Ages is generally perceived as backwards, relying on repugnant home remedies and prayers. To a certain extent this is true; but it's also true that physicians performed various ground-breaking operations and cures that are similar to many modern procedures. Brain surgery, anesthesia, cosmetic surgery and, to a degree, sterilization, were all practiced in the Middle Ages.

During the Dark Ages, the majority of classical writings on medicine were lost to most of the European continent. However, many of the Jewish and Moorish inhabitants of Spain continued to study and translate Greek manuscripts written by such physicians as Hippocrates, Galen, Anthimus and Aurelius Celsus.

Because of their knowledge of Arabic and usually Greek, Jewish doctors were considered by most people to be superior to other doctors. As a result, Jewish doctors traveled extensively from court to court where they were highly paid.

In northern Europe, most medicine was practiced and governed by the church, which thought illnesses were divine retribution. Inside each monastery and abbey, a monk was appointed "leech" to care for the sick.

Due to the belief that God had stricken them with their illness, many of the sick took pilgrimages in the hope of recovery by making peace with God. The more practical medicine for the masses was usually performed by women who relied on remedies passed down to them from elders. Aside from being well versed in herbs and poultices, women were also taught the benefits of massage. There is also evidence of women being licensed to practice medicine, and some women specialized in certain disorders such as eye diseases.

What few physicians and surgeons there were stayed predominantly in the cities, or in households of the wealthy where they received considerable wages and privileges. But buyer beware: charlatans abounded. Just like today, the type and quality of care each doctor provided depended on his own philosophy and where he had studied his craft.

Even though the majority of northern Europe was Christian, many pagan cures, incantations and spells were still used by women and doctors. These were forbidden by the church and, as a result, many archaic spells were given a more Christian flavor; instead of invoking the pagan gods, the Christian God and his saints were called upon. Astrology and numerology were practiced as a vital part of medicine until modern times.

The first medical university was founded in the tenth century in Salarno, Italy. Schools in Montpellier, Bologna, Padua and Paris soon followed. The length of the medical programs varied greatly. In order to be declared a Master, a student had to prove himself able to debate, lecture and recite the content of his studies.

Even with the success of these universities, the church frowned on medical studies, and in 1139, the Second Lateral Council banned the use of bodies for temporal knowledge. Despite the church's authority, the university had passed into secular control, and many students, teachers and physicians carried on their work by using the bodies of pigs and executed convicts. In the fourteenth and fifteenth centuries, the church ruled against surgery and only a small number of medical students were allowed to attend dissections. France, in the fourteenth century, began prosecuting unlicensed practitioners of medicine, including women.

One of the most important achievements of the Middle Ages was the invention of the hospital. These were set up by the church, but were not for the blind, pregnant, crippled, orphaned, leprosy or plague victims. They were for the wounded and "regular," hopefully curable, sick.

The most common diseases were dysentery, epilepsy, influenza, diphtheria, scurvy, typhoid, St. Vitus' Dance, St. Anthony's fire, smallpox, scabies, scrofula, impetigo, leprosy, pneumonia, stroke and heart attack.

Tuberculosis, cancer, alcoholism and venereal diseases were rarely recorded. Diseases such as polio, typhus, cholera, yellow fever, sleeping sickness, bronchitis and syphilis did not show up until the end of the period.

The insane were treated kindly in the Middle Ages and unless they were dangerous, they were allowed to roam about as they pleased. Some were taken in by almshouses. Since the insane were thought to be possessed, the only treatment for insanity was exorcism. Oftentimes, crosses were shaved into their heads. Many would be tied in church so they could hear mass and have the benediction of God. St. Vitus' Dance, which was most common during the fourteenth century, was treated by binding the victim in cloth to prevent him from harming himself—much like an early form of a straitjacket.

Lepers were ostracized from society and forbidden from entering a church, mill, tavern, bakehouse, from washing in a spring, stream or fountain, and from going near a large gathering of people. Some were allowed to live in leper colonies, while others roamed the countryside in perpetual pilgrimage. Laws required lepers to wear distinct clothes (black robe with white patches and a tall red hat), and they were required to signal their approach to other travelers with a set of wooden castanets. They were also required to remain downwind of any person they spoke to. Many people gave them free food and, for the most part, lepers were treated with compassion. But there were also times when fear gripped the people and lepers were hanged or burned.

Doctors were carefully taught how to tend patients. When a servant came to fetch a doctor, the doctor extracted a full report of the patient's symptoms from the servant so he could later astound the patient with his knowledge of the patient's condition.

Doctors were trained to put the patient at ease and to make jokes while they worked. One of the first duties of a doctor was to check the patient's urine for color and possible sediments. They would then taste the urine for sugar. During all procedures, doctors were to keep their hands clean and their nails well manicured.

Doctors believed in preventative medicine and advised people to take regular baths, refrain from naps, take a walk every day, heed nature's call immediately, watch their diets, try to be happy, and settle problems without letting them fester. The medieval doctor followed the Greek belief that the body was made up of four humors (sanguine, choler, phlegm and melancholia) and three spirits.

Though physicians were scholars who studied at the universities, surgeons belonged to the working class and did the jobs that were considered beneath the physician, such as bloodletting and pulling teeth. In fact, most surgeries were performed by the barber/surgeon. Surgical instruments included scissors, speculum, razor, scalpel, needle and lance. Some of the most common operations were for hernias, cancer, gallstones and cesarean sections.

Pregnant women were considered beneath the care of a doctor. When a woman went into labor, a midwife was called. Many medieval women gave birth in a sitting stance or in a birthing chair, which kept the mother standing and thereby allowed gravity to assist in the birth.

When a midwife was called, she would section off the lying-in chamber (all men were banned). The mother's belly was rubbed with a special ointment to help ease the pains. All closed objects in the house were opened, including knots left in ropes. This was believed to help ease the mother's pain.

After birth, the baby was washed and rubbed down with salt. His mouth would be cleansed with honey; then the babe was bound in tight swaddling.

If the child appeared to be dying, the midwife would christen it and sprinkle water on the infant as baptism. If the mother died, the midwife would perform a C-section and free the baby, or at the very least, christen and baptizing the child before it died.

DENTAL CARE

Though few and far between, dentists did exist in the Middle Ages and were called *dentatores*. Most dental science came to Europe from the Arabs, and rather advanced techniques were available.

Just like today, dentatores removed decay (which was thought to be caused by worms) and filled the cavities with ground bone. By the fifteenth century, gold fillings were used. Dentatores also repaired loose teeth with metal binders, and made dentures of ox bone and other various materials.

Only the very rich could afford the cost of real dentatores. The rest of the population had to rely on barbers to pull their teeth at a booth in a fair or market. Peasants usually pulled their own teeth.

Dental tools included scrapers, forceps, rasps, saws, spatumina, elevators, cauteries, probes, scalpels, tooth trephines and siles.

MEDICAL BREAKTHROUGHS

In the late ninth and early tenth centuries, Rhazes attempted cures for smallpox and measles and met with a small amount of success.

Guy de Chauliac (not to be confused with the later Guy de Chauliac from the fourteenth century) pioneered antiseptic surgery in the thirteenth century.

Mondin de'Luzzi wrote the first book of anatomy entitled *Anthania* in 1316. During the same time, Yperman began to feed patients artificially with a tube made from an esophagus.

In the fifteenth century, the Brancas performed successful cosmetic surgery by using skin grafts and bones to reconstruct ears, noses, lips and other body parts. Autopsies were performed to determine organ sizes and to help understand what had killed the victim in an effort to save the next stricken. It was also in the fifteenth century that scientists discovered that different parts of the brain controlled various functions of the body.

TREATMENTS

Ague: Wrap a spider in a raisin and swallow.

Ailments: Rubbing the boiled-down fat of a newly deceased felon on the troubled area cured most ailments.

Anesthesia: A sponge should be soaked in the juice of opium, morel, hyoscyamus, ivy, lettuce, mandragora, mandrake or hemlock and then dried in the sun. At the time of the surgery, the sponge should be resoaked in water and held to the patient's nose and mouth until he loses consciousness.

Baldness: Rub goose droppings over bald areas.

Broken Bones: If the bone has already begun to set, rebreak it and reset the bone to the correct position. The limb is then held by a splint or a plaster cast.

Bruises: Heat a large stone in a fire until it is scorching, then toss it in water and bathe the bruise twice a day. This speeds healing.

Burns: Take sheep's hard fat and boil with the rind from an elder tree. The ointment will cure a burn without leaving a scar.

Colds: Barley water: For each sextier of boiling water, add a rounded bowl of barley, two parisis of licorice and figs. Boil until the barley bursts. Strain with cloth and add crystallized sugar in each cup.

Coughs: Combine a quarter pint of vinegar with a quarter ounce of finely ground licorice. Heat until licorice dissolves. Add honey. Give a spoonful when cough is bad.

Cramps: Tie an eel skin around the knee.

Failing Mother's Milk: Boil peas, beans and gruel in milk and eat as a regular meal. Onions, garlic and heavily seasoned foods should be avoided.

Fevers: Boil a bit of barley, then strain out water. Place barley in more water and boil again. Strain one last time and add honey, then drink. Cold stream water may also be used.

Freckles: Cover the freckles with blood from a bull or a hare. Water distilled from expressed walnuts is also good.

Hemorrhages: Stave off blood flow by using stitches, binders or styptics.

Smallpox: Wrap the victim in red cloth and hang additional pieces of red cloth around the bed. This helps the victim recover sooner and reduces pockmarks.

Toothache: Touch a dead man's tooth.

Head Wound: Due to the number of head wounds sustained from battle and tourneying, trepanning was performed fairly often. Trepanning involves surgically cutting open the head with a scalpel or knife. The air of the operating room must be kept warm and hot plates are placed around the head to help keep it warm as well. Everything in the room and every instrument should be absolutely clean.

Wounds: Some wounds were cauterized, others could be treated with a strong cleansing of wine and then bound with clean cloth. The whites of new eggs were also rubbed across the wound to provide a soothing balm. Another cure was to hold the wound closed and chant, "In the name of the Father, Son and Holy Mary. The wound was red, the cut deep, the flesh be sore, but there will be no more blood or pain till the blessed Virgin bears a child again."

Common Remedies
Here's a list of items that were kept on hand and what they were used for.

Acorn: Placed in the middle of a window, it kept a house from being struck by lightning, and a woman who carried one would never age.

Adder Stone: If carried in the pocket, adder cured eye disorders.

Agate: Absorbed maladies. For example, if a fever raged, agate was placed over the forehead to draw out the fever. In the shape of a triangle, agate cured stomach pains, and if placed in a cup of water, a woman who drank it would be fertile.

Amethyst: Prevented drunkenness.

Blackberry: Relieved diarrhea.

Blackcurrant: Relieved sore throats.

Camphor: Warded off infections.

Dandelion: Acted as a laxative.

Golden Rod: Relieved vomiting and stomach upset.

Ground Ivy: Relieved ulcers.

Hop: Relieved stomach upset.

Horehound: Supressed coughing.

Jasper Stone: Eased labor pains and prevented pregnancy.

Juniper: Warded off demons and epidemics.

Marigold: Reduced fever.

Nettles: Relieved rashes.

Peppermint: Relieved gas.

Rosemary: Grew hair.

Rosewater: Relieved eye inflamation.

Sorrel: Reduced high fever.

Southernwood: Relieved menstrual cramps.

Wormwood: Prevented and relieved digestion problems.

Yarrow: Prevented colds.

FOR FURTHER READING

M. Bishop, *The Middle Ages.*
Culpeper's Color Herbal.
J. and F. Gies, *Life in a Medieval City.*
K. Haeger, *The Illustrated History of Surgery.*

F. Heer, *The Medieval World*.

Tony Hunt, *The Medieval Surgery*.

B. Inglis, *History of Medicine*.

D. Jacquart & C. Thomasset, *Sexuality and Medicine in the Middle Ages*.

P.M. Jones, *Medieval Medical Miniatures*.

L.C. McKinney, *Early Medieval Medicine*.

M. Pouchelle, *The Body and Surgery in the Middle Ages*.

J.M. Riddle, *Contraception and Abortion from the Ancient World to the Renaissance*.

M. Rowling, *Everyday Life in Medieval Times*.

N.G. Siraisi, *Medieval and Early Renaissance Medicine: an Introduction to Knowledge and Practice*.

C.H. Talbot, *Medicine in Medieval England*.

CHAPTER FOUR

ECONOMY

With the fall of the Roman Empire, the European economy reverted to a barter system. Though money continued to be minted and used, it wasn't until the twelfth century that a monetary system became fully functional.

Throughout the period, fairs and peddlers played an important role. During the early part of the period, the crumbling roads and uncertain times made for treacherous traveling, but even so, courageous merchants plied their trade. In the beginning, these merchants used mules and horses to carry their wares. Carts were usually reserved for farm work, and the disrepair of the early roads was such that carts turned over easily (a lord could claim the items that fell from someone else's cart or horse). Traveling merchants began using wagons in the twelfth century, and as their trade increased, lords began repairing and maintaining the roads on their lands. One rule of the road that all travelers followed was to take the left when they encountered oncoming travelers.

As the times settled, the fairs became even more essential to the medieval economy. With their popularity came a variety of taxes levied against merchants and travelers. Some lords even forced travelers to pay a tax for protection (something the traveler seldom received).

As trade surged in the eleventh century, guilds emerged (the clergy formed them a century earlier). Guilds regulated the quality and price of their trades. Apprentices were signed on early in life for a period of seven years at which point they could become journeymen or journeywomen. Depending on their contracts, they might have to pay their master a small or large fee before leaving the house. Women apprentices usually stayed on with their master

47

until they married. To gain guild mastership, journeymen/women had to produce a masterpiece of workmanship. If the guild deemed it worthy, they became masters.

Though there were a number of female-dominated guilds such as weaving, brewing and spinning, most of these were overseen by men. The guilds provided a modicum of protection for workers much like a modern union, but for a variety of reasons not all occupations formed guilds.

The reasons for guilds are multitudinous. Guilds gave the towns power to barter their freedom from the lords or king who ruled them and allowed them to form their own laws. As a result of this power, there were also towns who never had guild merchants. Some lords refused to relinquish control.

Guilds traditionally aligned themselves to the church and chose a patron saint. Most of them held religious ceremonies at the beginning of their meetings. But, as shown by Geoffrey Chaucer, religion was not always on their mind:

> *Wel semed ech of hem a fair burgeys*
> *To sitten in a yeldehalle on a deys.*
> *Everich, for the wisdowm that he kan,*
> *Was shaply for to been an alderman.*
> *For catel hadde they ynogh and rente,*
> *And eek hir wyves wolde it wel assente;*
> *And elles certeyn were they to blame.*
> *It is ful fair to be ycleped "madame,"*
> *And goon to vigilies al bifore,*
> *And have a mantel roialliche ybore.*

Translated:

> *Well it seemed each of them (the dyer, carpenter, weaver,*
> *carpet-maker and haberdasher) a fair burgess*
> *to sit in a guildhall on a dias.*
> *By their wisdom each of them*
> *could justify being an alderman.*
> *They had enough capitol and money,*
> *And each of their wives held their assent*
> *And if they didn't then they should*
> *It is full fair to be called madame*
> *And going to vigils before all*
> *And having your mantel carried like royalty.*

Again, people then as now were motivated by a gamut of reasons to participate in guilds and guild ceremonies. And the agenda and function of each guild depended on the aldermen leading it.

COINS

Bezant: European term for gold Byzantine coin until around 1030.

Denier: Worth one-twelfth of the sou.

Ducat: Venetian gold coin that dates around 1084.

Ecu: A gold coin minted by King Louis IX in 1266.

Farthing: Worth one-fourth of a penny.

Florin: Mid-twelfth century Florentine gold coin.

Gros: Worth a thick penny.

Gros Tournois: Worth a sou.

Gulden: German gold coin minted in the fourteenth century.

Halfpenny: Worth half a penny.

Hyperpyron: Name used after 1030 for the Byzantine gold coin.

Livre: Worth about twenty shillings.

Mark: Coin used throughout Europe. Its worth varied greatly (twelve shillings in England).

Noble: Gold coin in England minted in 1344. Worth half a mark.

Penny, Pence: Worth a penny.

Pound: Worth twenty shillings.

Shillings: Worth twelve pence.

Silver Denier: Eighth century coin used in France, Germany and Spain.

Solidi: Roman currency that faded out around 550.

Sou: Worth one-twentieth of a livre.

Sterling: Used postconquest.

Thrymsas: Saxon coins used around the seventh century.

FOR FURTHER READING

J.W. Baldwin, *The Medieval Theories of the Just Price, Romanists, Canonists and Theologians in the Twelfth and Thirteenth Centuries.*

A. Ballard, *The English Borough in the Twelfth Century.*

J.M. Bennett, E.A. Clark, J.F. O'Barr, *Sisters and Workers in the Middle Ages.*

C. Gross, *The Gild Merchant.*

Jacques Le Goff, *Time, Work, and Culture in the Middle Ages.*

——— *Your Money or Your Life: Economy and Religion in the Middle Ages.*

Henri Pirenne, *Medieval Cities: Their Origins and the Revival of Trade.*

J.W. Thompson, *Economic and Social History of the Middle Ages 300 to 1300* (2 vols).

G. Unwin, *The Gilds and Companies of London.*

R.C. van Caenegem, *The Birth of the English Common Law.*

CHAPTER FIVE

FAMILY

When two people married, they seldom lived at home with another family member. Most moved into their own household. Not even children usually inhabited the home. After the age of five, children of the noble class were usually sent either to a monastery or to live with another member of the nobility. In the middle class, children were apprenticed to a trade.

Living with another family, the child learned what it needed for adulthood. Girls might remain in the household that reared them until marriage. If a girl returned home, her stay was usually only long enough for a suitable marriage to be arranged. However, there are cases of women who did venture into trades on their own, but these were rare.

Sons would either stay in their current household or venture out to make their way in the world. Once the universities were founded, some boys studied there. Siblings rarely grew up together or even saw one another.

It is easy to think that this would make medieval families callous about one another; however, this is not true. Then as now, we see that families interacted in a variety of ways. Two cases are mentioned in the introduction to this book: the brothers who wrote home and the father who chastised his errant son. We also see mothers such as Eleanor of Aquitaine who remained close to her sons throughout her life. And even though marriages were traditionally arranged, again we see a number of love matches made.

Children sent away usually came home a few times a year to visit their parents and they continued this practice even after they reached adulthood. Siblings would also visit one another with some regularity, and there are cases of brothers living together until marriage.

It is very difficult to draw generalizations about how the average family behaved and interacted during this time. As today, a gamut of attitudes about education, parental responsibility and teaching morals existed. Most parents tried to do their best by their children, but to say every parent held only their child's best interest at heart would be erroneous. Like a modern parent, Charlemagne refused to allow his daughters to marry because he didn't want to lose his "precious angels." Yet there are many cases of parents tossing their children out to make their own way.

We can no more draw an average family and how they interacted in the Middle Ages than we can about families today. Yes, a large percentage of our modern families go to church, but some go on Saturday, some on Sunday, some on Wednesday nights, some on Tuesday or Thursday nights and some every night of the week. Some parents refuse to punish their children and others beat them. Some children hate their parents and some parents hate their children. Some children are studious and others are not. Some parents encourage children to study and others don't. All these variables and more also existed in medieval families.

Children were taught to love and honor their parents but as Barbara Hanawalt points out in her book *Growing up in Medieval London*, "Children . . . might repay their parents and stepparents with lawsuits and beatings, rather than with respect and thanks."

Indeed, in my research I am more often stunned by the similarities of medieval society to the present than I am by the differences. To such an extent, we see many manuscripts written as instruction to parents on how to rear their children. Advice from medieval Dr. Spocks permeates middle- and upper-class society. Everything from manners to health to appropriate punishments are included. Many times these concur, but there are also differing views on what is appropriate.

During the millennium that makes up the Middle Ages, a wide variety of attitudes are found. For this reason, I urge researchers to focus on books written to specific time frames and countries, and to draw as few generalizations as possible.

❧ ❧ ❧

FOR FURTHER READING

Michael Altschul, *A Baronial Family in Medieval England.*
Philippe Aries, *Centuries of Childhood: A Social History of Family Life.*
John Boswell, *The Kindness of Strangers.*
J.A. Brundage, *Law, Sex and Christian Society in Medieval Europe.*
G. Duby and P. Aries, *History of Private Life.*
Georges Duby, *The Knight, the Lady and the Priest.*
————— *Medieval Marriage.*
Frances and Joseph Gies, *Marriage and the Family in the Middle Ages.*
Jack Goody, *The Development of the Family and Marriage in Europe.*
B.A. Hanawalt, *Growing up in Medieval London.*
Jacques Heers, *Family Clans in the Middle Ages.*
David Herlihy, *Medieval Households.*
Paul V.B. Jones, *The Household of a Tudor Nobleman.*
Kate Mertes, *The English Noble Household 1250 to 1600.*
S.M. Stuard, *Women in Medieval Society.*

CHAPTER SIX

WOMEN

The exact role of women in the Middle Ages is difficult to define. Researchers are bombarded by all sorts of contradictory attitudes. We see the writings of the church that instruct men to keep their wives and daughters far from the outside world and all its temptations. After all, they reasoned, women are weak-willed and less able than men to resist sin. Yet we also see writings that instruct women to help keep their husbands safe from sin, to care for the sick and indigent, and so on. Other laws say a woman cannot bring trial except for the killing of her husband or personal injury, but numerous cases are listed of women who brought trial for all sorts of reasons and who received judgments in their favor.

Just as you find today, there were women who were completely under the control of their husbands, and women who were their own lords and masters—women such as Adela of Blois who closed her gate to her husband and refused to allow him entry until the rest of the crusading knights returned home.

Historian Patricia Orr has even challenged the precept that all women were either married or waiting to be married. She believes far more women lived alone than has been previously suspected. For myself, I tend to uphold Eileen Power's belief of a "rough and ready equality between the sexes."

But one thing is clear: the role of a woman and her "value" changed throughout the period. In the early Middle Ages when there were more men seeking wives than there were women available for marriage, we find a "bride price" being paid for the woman. Women tended to marry later in life and had greater autonomy from their husbands. In Anglo-Saxon England, there is even a case of a former prostitute who was a major land-holding thane.

During the eleventh century, this balance began to shift. We see more cases of primogeniture (where one son inherits all) as opposed to consortial inheritance (where the land is split equally among children). Once this happened, the pool of men seeking wives shrank and the number of women seeking husbands grew. Suddenly, the value of a daughter dropped. Instead of a bride price, we find the father paying a dowry to rid himself of the daughter.

Some of these unwanted women were absorbed by convents, but with so few convents available and with the high entrance price a father had to pay to the convent, many women were left out. Since noblewomen couldn't enter the workplace and often couldn't enter a convent, they became unwanted burdens passed from one relative to the next. This has been proposed as one of the reasons for the rise of the Beguines in the thirteenth century.

But due to a scarcity of women on record, it is almost impossible even to guess at the number of women who did enter the workplace. As Monica Green has pointed out, there is only one midwife listed in medieval England. Are we then to believe that the whole of England had only one midwife? Of course not. The fact is, many women, whether noble or not, were never accounted for in medieval records.

But from the existing records, we see medieval women working as surgeons, warriors, leaders, eye specialists, journeywomen, peddlers and more. There is even a story of a woman who entered a university in the guise of a man.

Yet despite opportunities and certain powers, women were usually under the control of a male relative or husband. This doesn't mean women were completely bound to their men. First, the husband was often away for long periods of time (one case records the absence of a husband for over thirty years), and secondly, the husband had plenty of duties of his own without being bothered with things such as the hiring of tutors or gardeners, deciding how much cloth was needed from the fair, checking the quality of the butter, weaving cloth, and performing other household tasks.

After all, a medieval woman was a busy one. Peasant women worked alongside their families in the fields and performed other duties such as milking cows and providing labor. Middle-class women were responsible for the welfare and education of apprentices, especially the females. They also bought goods for the entire household, helped their husbands in their trade, watched the shop, distributed alms, and sometimes had a separate trade of their own.

Many women in the Middle Ages spent a good deal of time spinning and weaving cloth, among other duties.

Noblewomen oversaw the entire running of the estate: tilling the field, making candles, overseeing meals, directing servants and tithing, among other tasks.

An average day for a noblewoman might include attending morning mass, grabbing a quick bite to break the fast, meeting with servants to instruct them on special duties for the day, meeting with the steward and other officials, overlooking accounts and records, and breaking for the midday meal at noon. If guests were present, she'd spend the rest of the day entertaining them with hunting trips, hawking, singing, or some other planned festivity. Otherwise, she'd check on the servants, and make sure the children were attending their lessons. In the absence of her husband, she would also be expected to hear complaints and even rule in legal matters. In the event of an attack, she would lead the castle's defense.

❊ ❊ ❊

A woman wearing typical peasant garb of the Middle Ages.

FOR FURTHER READING

J.M. Bennett, E.A. Clark, J.F. O'Barr, B.A. Vilen, and S. Westphal-Wihl, eds., *Sisters and Workers in the Middle Ages*.

G.S. Burgess and K. Busby, trans., *The Lais of Marie de France*.

C.W. Bynum, *Holy Feast and Holy Fast: The Religious Significance of Food to Medieval Women*.

Christine de Pizan, *A Medieval Woman's Mirror of Honor*.

G. Duby and M. Perrot, *A History of Women: Silences of the Middle Ages*.

————— *A History of Women: From Ancient Goddesses to Christian Saints*.

Frances and Joseph Gies, *Women in the Middle Ages*.

N.L. Goodrich, *Priestesses*.

Tim Newark, *Women Warlords*.

Regine Pernoud, *Joan of Arc.*
Eileen Power, *Medieval Women.*
S.M. Stuard, *Women in Medieval Society.*
Barry Windeatt, trans., *The Book of Margery Kempe.*

CHAPTER SEVEN

FESTIVALS

estivals and holidays were celebrated many different ways. Just think about today's customs. Many people have a Christmas tree and exchange gifts, yet different families put their trees up and take them down on different days. How the tree is decorated also changes drastically from house to house. Some people exchange presents on Christmas eve and some on Christmas day. Some families eat turkey, others goose, and still others choose ham. The same variety existed in the Middle Ages.

The following is a general list of possible dates and celebrations. Remember, there were more than 126 holidays on the medieval calendar and some were celebrated and some weren't. Again, think of our own society—some people celebrate Columbus Day and others don't. Who celebrated the following days depended on what the holiday signified and the customs of the family, county and country.

✤ ✤ ✤

JANUARY 5

Twelfth Night: This celebration concludes the twelve days of Christmas. The festivities open with the choosing of a King and Queen of the Bean by serving two cakes—one to the men and one to the women. This may remind modern readers of the Mardi Gras cake, which contains a toy baby. But in this case, a bean, jewel or glass bead is inserted in the cake. The man and woman who receive the beans are declared king and queen. Once they are chosen, regardless of their social standing, they are seated at the high table and served as lord and lady of the hall.

During supper, six people disguised as oxen (complete with horns and bells), run in and dance around the wassail tree. Once they finish, the king and queen choose the "best beast" and a firm cake in the shape of a doughnut, or a papier mâché duplicate, is placed on its horn. The best beast then tries to shake off the cake without using any hands. The other dancers mimic the beast. The spectators watch and wager whether the cake will fall in front of or behind the beast.

When supper is finished, the celebrants gather to wassail (drink a toast to) the trees. They either go outside to the oldest tree or surround a tree placed in the hall. Some even assemble around mock trees made of subtleties or papier mâché. The celebrants gather around the tree and form a circle. They toast the tree with cider, and each cup contains three pieces of seed cake. After toasting, they eat one piece of cake, and offer the other two pieces to the tree. After this, they sing and circle the tree, then pour the rest of their cider at the tree's roots. With this done, they shout and make as much noise as possible.

Another important part of the celebration is the mumming. Plays and skits are acted out by performers, some of whom are noble, others of whom are not. They can be professionals, but usually the mummings are performed by locals. One type of mumming is the hobby horse. A highly decorated wire and straw frame surrounds a mummer who mimics a knight astride his stallion.

For the final event of the night, which is performed at midnight, all the candles are doused. Suddenly, a light appears. The light may be a candle on a long pole, or a lighted chandelier that is pulled along the top of the hall by a series of pulleys. Three actors follow the light and mum the play of the three magi. Once they defeat Herod, the revelers retire.

FEBRUARY 14

St. Valentine's Day: In a culture known for courtly love, it's easy to see how Valentine's day can have a special significance. The ways of celebrating varied, but almost everyone wore a symbol of love — a lover's knot, which is two circles side by side, a heart or a crowned A, which can either be pins or fabric that is pinned to the clothing. Sleeves could also be exchanged. In *The Canterbury Tales*, we see Chaucer's Prioress wearing a crowned A:

A piere of bedes, guaded al with grene,
And theron heng a brooch of gold ful sheene
On which ther was first write a crowned A,
And after Amor vincit omnia [love conquers all].

The hall is decorated with scented candles and hollowed out vegetables in which candles are placed. Often, a smile is carved into these lanterns. In addition to the usual trenchers, another trencher is added — one intended to be shared by lovers. Pairs are chosen by lot, then seated together. The food is served, but along with the usual feast a few special valentine foods are served, including heart-shaped cakes.

After supper, several games can be played. One favorite is to pass around yarrow sprigs. A healthy sprig means love eternal, and a wilting sprig signifies the recipient will never find true love. Another game is to place the sprig on a pillow, sprinkle it with rosewater and check it in the morning. Again, a wilted sprig means no love and a healthy one means eternal love.

MARCH (OR EARLY APRIL)

Easter: Beginning on Septuagesima and ending on Trinity day, the Easter celebration lasted approximately 120 days. Easter day is the first Sunday after the vernal equinox. An important part of this is Lent, which starts Ash Wednesday and ends on Easter day. During this forty-day period, no marriages can take place and fasting is expected.

During the Easter feast, plays and skits take center stage with skits of St. George and Noah being two favorites. Dancers also play an important role. They stamp about with wooden clogs in an effort to awaken the sleeping spring spirits.

One interesting addition to the table is the "pace eggs." These are eggs decorated like our Easter eggs, only they are placed in a centerpiece. A priest blesses the eggs. In parts of England, the eggs are exchanged between men and women, or are given to the mummers as pay.

APRIL 1

April Fool's Day: On April 1, it's the jester who rules the hall as the Lord of Misrule and on this day, everything is backwards (whiddershins). During the meal, the feasters try to outdo each other with ridiculous tales.

MAY 1

Mayday: This festival is the celebration of life and love, of procreation and renewal. One of the most glorious of the medieval holidays, Mayday is a time of games, song and revelry.

One of the most popular events of the Mayday festival was the Maypole dance.

The May Queen is chosen in a variety of ways—because she is most honored, most beautiful, and at times she is selected by the winner of a joust or tournament. Celebrants wear green sashes across their bodies or wreaths on their heads. Men and women dance around the maypole counterclockwise, singing. At the end of the song, they drop hands and hasten to gather May dew. The dew is rubbed into the skin to help the complexion. After this, greenery is collected to make wreaths that will later adorn the hall. Once the gathering is complete, the dancers return to do a stamping type of dance.

Games of all sorts are played, and tournaments are held. A feast finishes off the night where the foods are all green, including the trenchers.

JUNE 21

Midsummer Eve: Celebrated during the summer solstice, most of the festivities occur outdoors. Baal fires, or bonfires, are lighted and the celebrants dance around them. In parts of Brittany, it is rumored that a girl who dances around seven bonfires will be married within the year.

Again, mummers, acrobats and musicians play an important role. During the feast, special foods are served: destiny cakes, which are cakes shaped like various items; diviner eggs, which are raw eggs broken into a bowl and whose yolks will tell the breaker of something to come; cuckoo-foot ale (a carbonated drink made with ginger, basil and anise), which is accompanied by the cuckoo's song; and St. John's bread, which is made from locust seedpods. For the latter dish, the celebrants ask questions that start with "How many." To get the answer, they count the number of seeds in a bite of bread.

Another popular game is St. John's Wort, which is the same as the Valentine's day game of using a yarrow sprig to determine true love. A variation of this is counting the petals of the midsummer rose using our modern game of "He loves me, he loves me not."

Other customs include a quest for St. John's fern. The finder can become invisible at will. And, of course, there is the wet fire ceremony. This is performed by either carving a wish on a wooden boat, or writing it on a piece of paper and placing the paper on a boat. A lighted candle is set in the middle of the boat, then the boat is released in a stream or pool of water. If the boat makes it to the other side with the candle still lighted, the wish will be granted. If it sinks, or if the candle blows out, then the wish will be unfulfilled.

The feast ends with a dance called Threading the Needle, which is a line dance around the bonfire. When the dance is over, the people throw torches into the water and douse the fire.

JULY 15

St. Swithin's Day: This holiday celebrates the bounty of summer. As at other feasts, many courses are served, and dances, songs and plays are performed. The two main celebrations are: bobbing for apples and halving the apples. When the apple is halved, one half is dipped in yellow-dyed cream and the other is dipped in salt water. It is then passed among five people who share it.

Women wore garlands in their hair similar to the one shown here as part of their festival attire.

AUGUST 1

Lammas: The day starts by breaking up a one-year-old quarter loaf of bread and leaving it for the birds. In fact, bread plays a very important part in this holiday, and often entire courses consist of nothing but bread dishes. Lamb's Wool (a spicy cider with floating apples) is drunk.

Among the games played is Bring Home the Bacon in which married women compete to see who can take a negative, hypothetical situation that involves her spouse and turn it into a positive outcome. The wife with the most amusing answer that reaffirms her husband's goodness wins.

At the end of the feast, everyone is given a loaf of bread with a lighted candle in it. The guests form a circle and the steward leads them around the hall three times. The candles are snuffed and all but one-quarter of the bread is eaten. The remainder will be used the next year to feed the birds.

SEPTEMBER 29

Michaelmas: During this holiday, the local mayor or lord places a large glove atop a high pole to denote the fair's meeting ground. The booths are set up and the crowds gather around the glove. In order to participate in the fair, the merchants must promise to give a portion of their proceeds to charity.

For the feast, goose is served. After the twelfth century, ginger dishes also played an important part.

OCTOBER 25

St. Crispin's Day: Bonfires are lit and a feast is served.

OCTOBER 31

All Hallow's Even: A large candelabrum is placed in the center of the hall, or the central hall fire is lit. The feast is served with apples playing an important role. One tradition is to peel an apple in a spiral, then toss the peel over the left shoulder. When it lands, it forms the initial of the thrower's sweetheart.

Apple bobbing is another game. An apple is assigned the name of a possible lover. If the person gets the apple, he or she will get the lover. The apple can also be placed beneath a pillow at night in hopes the sleeper will dream of their love. They awake before dawn and sit outside and eat the apple. If they don't get cold, they will attain their desire.

Crowdie, a sweet apple cream dessert shared among six people, is also an important element. Inside the crowdie are placed two marbles, two rings and two coins. Whoever gets a coin will be rich; whoever gets a ring will be married; and whoever gets a marble will lead a cold, lonely life. If diners get nothing, their lives will be full of uncertainty.

NOVEMBER 1

All Saint's Day: Feast day to honor the saints.

NOVEMBER 2

All Soul's Day: Prayers are offered for the dead. Children go "a-souling" (door to door singing and asking for soul cakes.)

NOVEMBER 25

St. Catherine's Day: Wheel brooches are worn as reminders of the saint's death.

Important foods for the feast include Cathern Cakes, which are shaped like wheels, and Lamb's Wool, which is placed in a cathern bowl. After the feast, circle dances are performed.

DECEMBER 24 TO JANUARY 25

Christmas: This holiday begins on Christmas eve and runs to Twelfth Night. The number twelve plays an important role—there are twelve candelabrums, twelve kisses or gifts exchanged beneath the mistletoe, twelve wassailings, twelve courses, and twelve sprigs of holly per bunch. One necessity is the yule log, a log so large it will burn for the full twelve days.

Sweet foods are favored including Yule dolls (gingerbread people), frumenty, humble pie, posset, mince pie and pudding.

One late medieval ceremony is the Christmas Threshold. A green line is drawn around the hall and the feast cannot begin until the "lucky bird" steps over the threshold. The lucky bird is a dark-haired man who wears green clothes and bells. With a leaping dance, he crosses the threshold and tips his cap to the high table where the feasters give him coin for good luck. He then goes from table to table collecting money.

The feast begins with a highly decorated and carefully carved yule candle being placed on the high table. Between courses, games and music are played. Hoodman's Bluff is one favorite game. As in the modern Blind Man's Bluff, a person is chosen and blindfolded, then turned around several times. He or she must capture another player and correctly identify the person. When the person is identified, the captured person becomes the hoodman.

Wassailing the Milly is also performed. This is done with singers or musicians who circle the hall singing carols and carrying a box that contains the Virgin and Child. Gifts are placed in the box as an offering, and at the end the gifts are given as alms to the poor.

GAMES

Other games that were played throughout the period for all sorts of holidays and celebrations include the following:

Hot Cockles: A rough little game where a lady or gentleman is blindfolded, then kneels. Celebrants take turns hitting the person on the head, trying to knock him or her over until the blindfolded person can identify the aggressors.

Ragman's Roll: Character traits or a fortune are written on parchment and sealed. People pull the seal or ribbon that dangles from the parchment and read aloud what is said about them.

FOR FURTHER READING

M.P. Cosman, *Fabulous Feasts: Medieval Cookery and Ceremony.*
——————— *Medieval Holidays and Festivals: A Calendar of Celebrations.*
M. Collins and V. Davis, *A Medieval Book of Seasons.*
P.H. Ditchfield, *Old English Customs.*
Dorothy Hartley, *Lost Country Life.*
Nigel Pennick, *The Pagan Book of Days.*
Dorothy Spicer, *Yearbook of English Festivals.*
Barbara Swain, *Fools and Folly During the Middle Ages and Renaissance.*

CHAPTER EIGHT

MUSIC

From the Gregorian chants, named after Pope Gregory the Great, to the haunting sound of bagpipes drifting over the moors before battle, music played an essential role in medieval life, especially since only a few pieces of literature were meant for silent reading. Almost all writings were designed to be sung.

Throughout the Middle Ages, jongleurs roamed about delighting castle and plain folk with their ballads, chansons de geste and lais. Rare was the castle meal that wasn't followed by a paid musician or a song. Music and dancing also are an important part of feasts and holidays.

Even the church, which threatened its clerical members with excommunication should they dance—especially on holy days—relaxed its laws and permitted the clergy to dance at Christmas, St. Catherine's Day and St. Nicholas's Day.

Medieval church music was delightful in its complex melodies and sweet a cappella style that echoed through the vaulted ceilings of the cathedrals. For small churches, music consisted of uncomplicated canticles and organums.

As a staple of courtly love, music and poetry were practiced by nearly all the noble class, and became a new occupation for the poorer classes. Women were expected to be accomplished musicians, and if a lady could compose, so much the better.

Jongleurs preferred to sing tales of King Arthur and his knights, deeds from the Holy Land, and songs of the Carolingian period. During the reign of Charlemagne, church officials warned jougleurs that they would be damned for their pagan songs that glorified heathen heros, but the church extolled songs that promoted God and Christianity, and even used them for missionary purposes.

A traveling musician in traditional garb. He holds a rebec.

However, the church didn't hesitate to preach against dance, using parables to dissuade people from doing it. In the parable of the Dancers of Colbek, a group decides to dance in a churchyard on Christmas eve and is punished by being made to dance in their spots until the Archbishop of Cologne releases them the following year.

Unfortunately for modern researchers, most songs were never written down, and since the first musical staff didn't appear until the late twelfth century, what little we have exists without the accompanying instrumental chords.

✤ ✤ ✤

DANCE

The medieval fixation with dance is evidenced by the wide variety of manuscript illuminations that survive and by a number of church writings that caution against the sinfulness of dance. Despite the church's condemnation, dancing remained a favorite pastime even among nuns and even at the threat of excommunication. Especially during the plagues, people spent many hours singing and dancing in an effort to forget their sorrows and enjoy what they feared were their last days.

Three dances have come down to us: the solo, the line/round/carol/ring (the terms are used interchangeably), and couples. Unfortunately, the exact steps aren't known, but from manuscript pages we know that round (ring) and line (carol) dances were performed by groups of people executing exact steps and holding hands in a circle or line as the name suggests. The accompanying dance songs were rotundellus (for a round dance), ductia and stantipes (for an estampie type of couples dance).

During dancing and celebrations—especially those held during tournaments—it wasn't uncommon for lords and ladies of the later Middle Ages to change their clothes three or four times a night. Another interesting game that came up in the High Middle Ages was *disguising*, which consisted of a group of masked people who ran into the great hall, performed a dance or song, and ran out as quickly as they had appeared.

TYPICAL INSTRUMENTS

Bagpipes (Scotland): Similar to the modern instrument. Originally used only as an instrument of war.

Bells: Shaken or struck with a hammer.

Buisine: A large horn with a turned-up bell.

Buccinal: A type of trumpet.

Buinne (Ireland): A reed instrument.

Chalumele: An oboe-like instrument.

Clarion or Claro: A trumpet that was played like a bugle and was approximately one meter long.

Clochetes: Small bells.

A musician plays a lute.

Cor: A hunting horn.

Cuisle (Scotland): A type of flute.

Cymbalum: Another name for bells.

Double Flute: A pan-like instrument usually made from reeds.

Estive: A type of bagpipe.

Fiddel: Similar to today's violin.

Fipple Flute (Ireland): A type of flute.

Flaute: A type of eight-holed flageolet.

Frestelles: Flute that resembled panpipes.

Gemshorn: A hollowed-out animal horn played like a flute.

Gigue: A tenor viele that was played like a violin or cello.

Harp: Similar to the modern instrument.

Hirgorn (Welsh): A trumpet.

Hurdy-gurdy: Similar to a violin, it was held on the knee and a wheel was rotated to make the sound. Buttons were pressed to hold down strings and chords. The first hurdy-gurdy had to be played by two people. After the twelfth century they were redesigned for one player.

Lute: A pear-shaped guitar-like instrument that had anywhere from four to twelve strings. The tuners are turned back from the neck at a ninety-degree angle.

Mandola: A larger version of the mandolin.

Mandore: A type of mandolin that was played on the lap.

Monicorde: An organ-like instrument played by two people.

Muse: A type of bagpipe.

Nakers: A double drum used by the Saracens and played by beating the skin with two drumsticks.

Pibau (Welsh): Bagpipes.

Pibgorn (Welsh): A reed instrument.

Pipai (Ireland): Bagpipes.

Psalterion: A zither that was held to the chest and plucked.

Rebec: A pear-shaped guitar-like instrument that occasionally had frets.

A musician with rebec, bagpipes, and a drum painted with a Celtic design.

Recorder: Similar to the modern version.

Rote: A five-string harp.

Shawm: Similar to today's oboe, it was favored by the Saracens and used as a battle instrument.

Stoc, Sturgen (Ireland): A trumpet.

Straight Trumpet: A long trumpet, usually over two meters long, and similar to a bugle.

Tamborine: Identical to today's version. Used by traveling minstrels for songs and dances.

Tinne (Ireland): A type of bagpipe.

Tiompan, Tympanum (Scotland): A harp-like instrument.

Telyn (Celtic): A type of harp.

Viele: A fiddle with a flat bottom.

FOR FURTHER READING

J. Arnold, *Medieval Music*.

J.W. Baldwin, *The Scholastic Culture of the Middle Ages 1000-1300*.

J. Cummins, *The Hawk and the Hound, the Art of Medieval Hunting*.

G. Duby, *The Age of Cathedrals*.

Gerald of Wales, *The Journey Through Wales*.

P.W. Hammond, *Food and Feast in Medieval England*.

U.T. Holmes, Jr., *Daily Living in the Twelfth Century*.

R.H. Hoppin, *Anthology of Medieval Music*.

C. MacKinnon, *Scottish Highlanders*.

E. Power, *Medieval People*.

Available Recordings

Paul Andrews, *Russian Church Music*.

Anonymous 4, *An English Ladymass*.

Baltimore Consort, *On the Banks of Helicon: Early Music of Scotland*.

Chant School of Munsterschwarzach Benedictine Abbey, *Death and Resurrection: Gregorian Chants for Good Friday, Easter Sunday, and Ascension Day*.

Joel Cohen, *Lo Gai Saber, Troubadours et Jongleurs 1100 to 1300*.

Folger Consort, *A Medieval Tapestry: Instrumental and Vocal Music from the 12th through the 14th Centuries*.

Ensemble Alcatraz, *Danse Royale*.

Joan Kimball and Robert Weimken, *Keeping the Watch and Return of the Pipers*.

Sister Mary Keyrouz, *Byzantine Chant*.

David Munrow, *Music of the Crusades*.

David Munrow, *Music of the Gothic Era*.

David Munrow, *The Pleasures of the Royal Courts*.

Marcel Peres: Ensemble Organum, *Chants of the Roman Church*.

Peter Phillips, *William Byrd: The Great Service*.

Peter Phillips, *Thomas Tallis: Lamentations of Jeremiah*.

Salve Regina, *Gregorian Chant*.

Wim Van Gervan, *Gregorian Chant*.

Compilations

Orthodox Liturgies.

The Tradition of Gregorian Chant

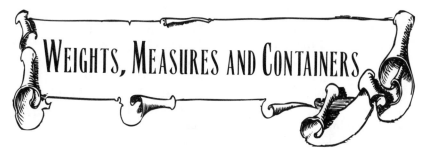

CHAPTER NINE

WEIGHTS, MEASURES AND CONTAINERS

The following is a list of common weights, containers and measures used in daily life during the Middle Ages. I should mention, however, that these weights and measures varied greatly not only from country to country, but even from village to village. The first mention of standard units of measure in England appears at the very end of the twelfth century. These measures were set either in stone or in metal, and they were kept under lock and key by a local official. Yet even so, the exact measure was often modified to conform to local tradition or expectation.

Once a "standard" was set, copies would be made available to the general public and the guilds. Again, they could and often were modified by whomever was using them for a variety of reasons. The guilds tried to regulate measurements and weights, as did local authority, and to hold merchants, craftsmen and traders accountable for any infringements, especially those who cheated clients. However, plenty of complaints were brought before local courts by outraged patrons who felt they didn't receive their money's worth.

❧ ❧ ❧

MEASURES:

Barrel = 30 to 32 gallons
Boll = 6 bushels
Bushel = 8 gallons
Butt = 2 hogshead
Cable = 120 fathoms
Cubit = 18 inches
Dram = 60 grains

Ell = 4 feet
Fathom = 5½ yards
Firkin = ¼ barrel
Firlot = ¼ boll
Fortnight = 2 weeks
Furlong = 220 yards
Gill = ¼ pint

Hand = 4 inches
Hogshead = 2 barrels
Kilderkin = ¼ tun
League = 3 miles
Noggin = ¼ pint
Pace = 2½ feet
Palm = 3 inches
Peck = 2 gallons
Pipe = ½ tun
Pole = 6 feet

Puncheon = 72 gallons (ale) or 84 gallons (wine)
Rod = 6 feet
Runlet = large runlet = 12 to 18½ gallons; small runlet = 1 pint to 4 gallons
Sennight = 1 week
Span = 9 inches
Tun = 252 wine gallons

WEIGHTS

Burthen = 70 pounds
Clove = 7 to 10 pounds
Fardel = 4 cloves
Firkin = 56 pounds
Grain = .0001736 of a pound
Hundredweight = 112 pounds

Kip = ½ ton
Pennyweight = 24 grains
Pound or Pounde = 317¼ grams
Stone = 14 pounds

CONTAINERS

Aquamanile: A water bowl used for washing hands.

Beaker: A tall, wide-mouthed goblet.

Blackjack: A large jug used to drink beer. Usually made of leather and coated on the outside with tar.

Costrel or Pilgrim's Bottle: A bottle or barrel with two ears on each side so it could be attached to the waist with string.

Ewer: A pitcher with a wide spout.

Flagon: A bottle that had a screw top or a lid.

Flasks: A container made of skin, bladder or any other material that could carry liquid.

Goblet: A bowl-shaped cup that lacked handles and had a base or stem. Usually made from glass or metal.

Horn: A drinking vessel made from the horns of various animals. Used throughout the period, especially by the Vikings and Saxons.

Mazer: A bowl, cup or goblet that lacked a stem and that was usually made of precious metal and elaborately decorated.

Mortar: Used for cooking or grinding medicines. A deep bowl made of hard materials such as rock or marble.

Phial: Any type of bottle that held liquids.

Piggin: Used as a milking pail or a drinking vessel, a piggin was a round bucket with one wooden piece longer than the rest, which was used as a handle. A bowl with a ladle was also called a piggin.

Pipkin: Mostly used for cooking, it was a small earthenware pot.

Rummer: A large drinking vessel, usually made of glass.

Stein: A large earthenware beer mug.

Tankard: In the earlier Middle Ages it was a tub-like vessel used to carry water. After the high Middle Ages, it became a tall, one-handled mug or cup that was used to drink beer and often came with an attached lid.

Tumbler: A pointed or round-bottomed drinking cup that couldn't be set down until empty.

Vial: A small- or medium-sized vessel that held liquids.

CHAPTER TEN

VOCABULARY

The following is a list of common medieval terms that may add flavor to dialogue or narrative. I would caution writers from making characters' dialogue too medieval. After all, there is a reason why the works of Shakespeare, Beowulf and Chaucer are not considered leisure-time reading by the majority of people. If you overuse terms and make the language too thick, you will alienate many readers.

❧ ❧ ❧

Aid: A financial obligation the vassal owes his lord for special circumstances or occasions.

Anon: At once or soon.

Armoyer: Armorer.

Aye, Yea: Yes.

Bannerets: Knights who were knighted on the battlefield and allowed to carry banners.

Benefice: A grant of land made by a lord.

Carona: Chandelier.

Castle Guard: A guard in a lord's castle.

Cauda: The train of a gown.

Chevauchee: Duty owed to the lord to serve as an escort.

Coffyn: The pastry around a pie.

Cornettes: Two-pointed headdress.

Courlieu: Private messenger.

Coz: Cousin.

Craft: A skilled labor.

Curia Regis: Royal council and court of justice.

Daub: Clay and hair smeared over the wooden structure of a house.

Demesne: Land held directly by the lord.

Eyre: English court.

Fief, Feud: Land held from a lord.

Fisyk: Medicine.

Flail: A stick used to separate wheat grains from ears.

Frankpledge: A pledge made by all the members of a community in which they vowed to take responsibility for their actions. If one person broke the law, all were responsible for bringing that person to justice.

Free-lance: A term used for mercenaries.

Givre: A lethal snake.

Grand Assize: Introduced in 1179, this law settled land disputes by a jury trial of twelve men rather than by Trial by Combat.

Hallmote: A manorial court.

Heriot: A death tax paid by the murderer if someone was killed.

Hither: Here.

Honor: The estate of a tenant-in-chief.

Host: Military service owed to a lord.

Journeyman, Journeywoman: A skilled worker who was employed by guildmasters or who worked independently for daily wages.

Knave: A disrespectful form of address to a man.

Knotty-pated, Addle-pated: Stupid.

Ling: A type of fish.

Lingulae: The keys on an organ.

Manches: Long, flowing sleeves.

Manor: Land held by a lord and worked by tenants.

Marcher Lord: Lord of a border region.

Nay: No.

Oblate: Someone who entered the church at an early age.

Oblation: A fee paid to the church by someone who gave their child to the clergy.

Outremer: The Holy Land.

Panoply: A soldier's equipment.

Parage: The feudal term for a younger brother who held lands from an older brother.

Parole: The word of honor given by a prisoner that he would not try to escape.

Peddler: A traveling salesperson.

Pullet: A young chicken.

Rag-picker: The lowest of the middle class.

Randy: Promiscuous.

Relief: Tax paid by the inheritor of an estate.

Rogue: Vagrant.

Rota: Chandelier.

Rushes: Marsh plants that were dried and used in a variety of ways.

Rushlight: A torch made from rushes.

Sally: Counterattack.

Scutage: The money paid to an overlord to get out of military service. This was also paid by the church, women and minors who were unable to perform the required military service their vassalage demanded. Existed as early as 1100.

Shandy: Stupid.

Simpkin: A fool.

Sirrah: A derogatory way to address a man.

Sister: The wife of a guildmaster who was allowed to enter the guild.

Span: The term for preparing a crossbow to be shot.

Stew: A brothel.

Stewholder: A brothel owner.

Tallow: A type of candle made from animal fat.

Thee: You. Used as an object for familiar people and social equals.

Thine: Yours. Used for social equals and friends.

Thither: There.

Thou: You. Used as a subject for social equals and familiar people.

Thy: Your. Used for social equals and friends.

'Tis: The contraction of it is.

Tourney: A tournament, especially a melee.

'Twas: The contraction of it was.

'Twill: The contraction of it will.

'Twould: The contraction of it would.

Vassal: A servant who had sworn allegiance to an overlord.

Vavasour: The lowest vassal on the French scale.

Villein, Serf: One who owed labor to a lord and was not a free man.

Wench: A disrespectful term for a woman.

Yon: That.

Zounds: God's wounds. Used as a mild oath.

... li ... sor chauule ....
... dont ... biaus sanit .
a uestu et aparellie se li ...
mor sir . cil . et il li fist ...
... au siege pullens . de le ...
... et bueue le diar dont il ...
... n uuir fere ... le ...
... fer a ... ...
... regart les letres ...
... le nom a ...
... Sir . cil . a ... ne
... ... la fist rot ...
... apres ome ... ...
... ana fer et ... ...
... ua mo . ...

PART TWO

Rank & Privilege

Chapter Eleven

Kings

n this chapter you will find a list of the kings who reigned in the British Isles during the Middle Ages or who reigned in countries that played an important role in the evolution of the British Isles. As you will see, a wide variety of men occupied the throne. Some were strong leaders who cared deeply for their country and who took seriously the responsibilities of the position. These kings improved—or at least attempted to improve—the lives of the people they ruled. Others were weak leaders who buckled to the demands of the time and place. Often these weak kings occupied the throne for short periods of time, unless they were supported by powerful behind-the-scenes forces. Still other kings were corrupt, assuming the throne solely for the power it brought them. These kings cared little for their people and often undid the achievements made by their predecessors. In short, kings in the Middle Ages were much like leaders today: human beings, capable of noble as well as ignoble deeds.

Before moving into the overview of the kings, I should mention that in England and Scotland, the line of succession to the throne is not difficult to follow. Norway, Ireland and Wales, however, frequently fought among themselves and with other countries throughout the period, so the title of king was a tenuous or, in many cases, a nonexistent one. Due to the confusing nature of the reigns of kings in these countries, a quick reference list is provided.

❊ ❊ ❊

ENGLAND

Alfred the Great 871 to 899: Approximately twenty-three years of age when crowned in 871, Alfred fought against the Danes and won several important battles before designing a truce (called the Danelaw) that sectioned off the Danes into Mercia, Northumbria and East Anglia. With the Danes quelled, he set about uniting and educating England, which became a reality during his son Athelstan's reign. He died of an unknown illness October 26, 899.

Edward the Elder 899 to 925: Coronated June 8, 900, at Kingston-on-Thames. His kingship was contested by Ethelwold, but Edward defeated him in 909. A renowned fighter, he renewed conflict with the Danes in 909. He died July 17, 924.

Aethelstan 925 to 939: Coronated September 5, 925, at Kingston-on-Thames. Handsome and blond, he succeeded in bringing together all the British races. He also raised Haakon Haraldsson (son of the first king of Norway) in his court. He died at age 44 from a mysterious illness.

Edmund I (the Magnificent) 939 to 946: Coronated November 16, 939, at Kingston-on-Thames at age eighteen. He allied England to Malcolm I of Scotland by giving Malcolm control of Strathclyde. By age twenty-four, he ruled over a peaceful Britain. He was killed while trying to subdue the outlaw Liofa in May 946.

Edred 946 to 955: Coronated August 16, 946, at Kingston. Like his brothers before him, he was plagued by the Danes and defeated them. He died around age thirty-two on November 23, 955.

Eadwig or Edwy the Fair 955 to 959: Coronated at age fourteen or fifteen, January 956 at Kingston. He was called the Fair as a result of his renowned handsomeness. Due to conflicts, he lost kingship of the North and Midlands. He died before his twentieth birthday.

Edgar the Peaceful 959 to 975: Coronated 973. He divided the shires into royal hundreds for legal purposes and gave considerable freedom to the English Danes. He stood less than five feet tall and had a peaceful reign. He died July 8, 975.

Edward the Martyr 975 to 979: Coronated at age fifteen in 975 at Kingston. His reign was short and ended in a brutal murder commissioned by his stepmother on March 18, 979.

Ethelred II (the Redeless or Unready) 979 to 1013, 1014 to 1016: Coronated at age ten on April 14, 979. His reign was plagued by problems, especially in dealing with the Danes. In 1013, he was deposed by Sweyn Forkenbeard. While under exile, he journeyed to

Normandy where he met and married Emma, the daughter of Richard I, Duke of Normandy (an event that set up William I's claim to the English throne in 1066). In 1014 Sweyn died and Aethelred returned to the throne until his death in 1016.

Sweyn Forkbeard 1013-1014: His reign of England was only six months. He died February 3, 1014.

Edmund II (Ironside) April to November 1016: Coronated in 1016 at St. Paul's Cathedral. Son of Ethelred, he was locked in a fight with Canute and ended up dividing England with him. Edmund took Wessex and gave Mercia to Canute. He died November 30, 1016.

Canute (Cnut, Knute) 1016 to 1035: Coronated January 6, 1016, at St. Paul's Cathedral. In 1019, he also became King of Denmark. Throughout his reign, Canute spent much of his time traveling between his lands in Denmark and England. He died November 12, 1035.

Harold I (Harefoot) 1035 to 1040: Coronated in 1035 to rule jointly with his brother Hardicanute. Since Hardicanute remained occupied in Denmark and couldn't make a trip to England, Harold was coronated as sole king in 1037 at Oxford. He died March 17, 1040.

Hardicanute (Hardicnut) 1040 to 1042: Coronated June 18, 1040, at Canterbury. Ruthless, he imposed severe taxes against the English natives and won their hatred. He died June 8, 1042.

Edward the Confessor 1042 to 1066: Coronated April 3 (Easter), 1043, at Winchester Cathedral. His reign was a welcomed change from the abuses of Hardicanute. He built Westminster Abbey and died not long after it was consecrated (January 5, 1066).

Harold II (Godwineson) January to October 1066: Coronated in 1066 at Westminster Abbey. He is described as tall and blond by the Anglo-Saxon *Chronicle*. His short reign was plagued by William the Bastard of Normandy and Harold Hardrada of Norway who both swore the throne belonged to them. He died at the Battle of Hastings, September 29, 1066.

William I (the Conqueror, the Bastard) 1066 to 1087: Coronated December 25, 1066, at Westminster Abbey. His early reign was plagued by rebellions, which he eventually quelled. He introduced and perfected the feudal system and building stone castles. Always a man of portly stature, he was described as tall and ruddy complected. He died September 8, 1087.

William II (Rufus) 1087 to 1100: Coronated September 26, 1087, at Westminster Abbey. Rufus comes from his red hair and ruddy complexion. An active soldier, he campaigned in Normandy. He died in a reputed hunting accident in New Forest on August 2, 1100.

Henry I (Beauclerc, Lion of Justice) 1100 to 1135: Coronated on August 6, 1100, at Westminster Abbey. He created a menagerie that can be viewed as the first English zoo. Constantly traveling from Normandy to England, he died in Normandy on December 1, 1135.

Stephen 1135 to 1154: Coronated December 26, 1135, at Westminster Abbey. He usurped the throne from his cousin Matilda. This caused a civil war from 1139 until 1152 when he and Matilda's son Henry signed the Treaty of Westminster, which allowed Stephen to reign and set up Henry as his heir. He died October 25, 1154.

Henry II (Plantagenet, Curtmantle) 1154 to 1189: Coronated December 19, 1154, at Westminster Abbey. Red-haired and gray-eyed, he was said to seldom remain still. Henry II instigated the precept of our modern legal system and returned order to the anarchy that had reigned alongside Stephen. His later reign was plagued by the rebellion of his sons and the queen. He died July 6, 1189.

Richard I (Lion Heart) 1189 to 1199: Coronated July 6, 1189, at Westminster Abbey. He spent most of his time in the Holy Land on crusade. In fact, he even married his bride in Cyprus in 1191. He died April 6, 1199.

John (Lackland) 1199 to 1216: Coronated May 27, 1199, at Westminster Abbey. Plagued by conflicts with Philip Augustus of France and Pope Innocent III (which resulted in excommunication of John and an interdict against all church services in England), John was forced to sign the Magna Carta in 1215. He died October 18, 1226.

Henry III 1216 to 1272: Coronated October 28, 1216, at Gloucester Cathedral and again May 17, 1220, at Westminster Abbey after squelching the civil war between the king and rebel barons. He didn't formally rule until 1227. Civil war again broke out due to Henry's favoritism with foreigners and his weak policies. He died November 16, 1272.

Edward I (Longshanks) 1272 to 1307: Coronated August 19, 1274 (he was in Sicily at the time of his father's death and didn't return home until 1274), at Westminster Abbey. He believed in and encouraged a parliamentary system and also implemented castle building in Wales. During his conflicts with Scotland, he took the Stone of Scone (the stone upon which all Scottish Kings had been coronated) and had the English Coronation Chair made to house it. He died July 7, 1307.

Edward II 1307 to 1327: Coronated February 28, 1308, at Westminster Abbey. He succeeded in offending a number of his nobles with his favoritism toward Piers Gaveston, an indiscretion that caused Piers to be murdered and Edward to be ultimately deposed by his wife.

Edward III 1327 to 1377: Coronated February 27, 1377, at Westminster Abbey. Claiming the title of King of France in 1340, he set off the Hundred Years War with France. A tall, regal man, he had constant, heated tantrums. During his reign, English became the national language and parliament became two separate houses. He died June 21, 1377.

Richard II 1377 to 1399: Coronated July 16, 1377, at Westminster Abbey. A tragic figure, he started out a year before his reign by meeting Wat Tyler and placated the peasant uprising. Unfortunately, this was the last great thing he did. He was deposed September 29, 1399, and died January 6, 1400.

Henry IV (of Bolingbroke) 1399 to 1413: Coronated October 13, 1399, at Westminster Abbey. He deposed Richard and seized the crown. Portly, he sported a beard and red hair. His reign was troubled by wars, one of which was fought against Owen Glendower and his battle for Welsh independence. He died as prophesied March 20, 1413.

Henry V 1413 to 1422: Coronated April 9, 1413, at Westminster Abbey. He continued his father's wars in Wales and France, which culminated in the signing of the Treaty of Troyes that named him the Regent and heir of France. He died August 31, 1422.

Henry VI 1422 to 1461: Coronated November 6, 1429, at Westminster Abbey. Only eight-months old when he ascended the kinship (August 31, 1422), he wasn't crowned until age eight, and at age ten, he was crowned King of France. His reign saw the end of the Hundred Years War in 1453, which was shortly followed by the Wars of the Roses (1455 to 1489). He was deposed March 4, 1461, but returned to the throne October 3, 1470, as a figurehead. He was again deposed April 11, 1471, and was murdered as a prisoner in the Tower of London on May 21, 1471.

SCOTLAND

Malcolm II 1005 to 1034: Malcolm II established the approximate boundaries of modern-day Scotland by annexing the Lothians. To protect his grandson's (Duncan) inheritance, he murdered several men—one of whom had a daughter who later married MacBeth.

Duncan I 1034 to 1040: An impetuous young man, he had a stubborn prejudice that turned a number of his people against him. He was murdered over the above blood feud by MacBeth who then took the throne.

MacBeth 1040 to 1057: He was in turn murdered by Duncan's son.

Lulach (the Simple) 1057 to 1058: Deposed by Malcolm.

Malcolm III (Canmore) 1058 to 1093: Spent almost the whole of his reign in wars trying to annex North England, especially after the Norman conquest. He died fighting at Alnwick in 1093.

Donald (Ban) III 1093 to 1094: Took the throne from his brother, Duncan, who had been sent to the English court as a safeguard against Malcolm's attacks. William Rufus supported Duncan, and Donald was briefly deposed. He murdered his brother, then split Scotland with his nephew, Edmund. He was ultimately deposed and blinded by Edgar and died in 1099.

Duncan II 1094: Not long after gaining the throne, he was murdered by his nephew and Donald.

Edmund 1094 to 1097: After being deposed by Edgar, he became a monk.

Edgar 1097 to 1107: Since he relied on William Rufus's help to gain the throne, he was forced to acknowledge the English king as his superior.

Alexander I 1107 to 1124: Continued to follow homage to the English king.

David I 1124 to 1153: He expanded the boundaries of Scotland to include the English territories of Westmorland, Northumberland and Cumberland. He only acknowledged the English king as sovereign for his English holdings and brought into Scotland a number of Anglo-Norman friends.

Malcolm IV (the Maiden) 1153 to 1165: An ineffectual leader, he was forced to return all the lands David had won.

William I (the Lion) 1165 to 1214: Attempting to regain the lost English lands, he was captured and sent to Normandy where he had to pay homage to Henry II. After Henry's death, his rights of independence were sold to him by Richard, and in the Quitclaim of Canterbury, Scotland's independence was acknowledged by the English.

Alexander II 1214 to 1249: Returned Cumberland and Northumberland to England.

Alexander III 1249 to 1286: Brother-in-law to King Edward of England. With no more male heirs, his throne went to his daughter after he died in an accident.

Margaret 1286 to 1290: A child of no more than seven, she set sail from Norway to her new kingdom where King Edward had hopes she would marry his son and unite the two. Unfortunately, she died before reaching Scotland.

John Balliol 1292 to 1296: For two years, a number of claimants stepped forward. The top two contenders were Robert Bruce (grandfather of the more famous Robert Bruce) and John. With a trick of brilliance, Edward agreed to choose between them, provided whoever won swore homage to him. He chose John, then set about trying to force John to rebel against him (an act that would enable Edward to claim the Scottish lands). In 1295, John renounced England and set up an alliance with France. Edward attacked, occupied it and captured John.

Robert I (the Bruce) 1306 to 1329: Rocked by feuds in Scotland (especially the one with the Comyns), he narrowly missed death a number of times from the Scottish. After the death of Edward, he slowly succeeded in uniting Scotland and gaining independence. He died in 1329.

David II 1329 to 1371: Deposed by Edward Balliol, he fought a six-year war in an effort to regain his throne. He regained his title in 1340 and reigned until his death in 1371.

Edward Balliol 1332 to 1338: With help from the English, he deposed David, but was eventually forced to flee. He died in 1363.

Robert II (the Steward) 1371 to 1390: Nearly fifty-five years in age when he ascended, his reign was marked by problems.

Robert III 1390 to 1406: No better at ruling than his father, he allowed Scotland to fall into even more misrule.

James I 1396 to 1437: Though unpopular with several of his lords, James set about regaining Scotland. He was the victim of a conspiracy that ended in his death.

James II (Fiery Face) 1437 to 1460: Named Fiery Face due to a birthmark, he was six when he ascended to the throne. He regained much of what had been lost and squelched a number of enemies. He died by accident while trying to retake Roxburgh.

FRANCE

Pepin (the Short) 751 to 768

Charles (the Great, Charlemagne) 768 to 814

Louis (the Pious) 813 to 840

Lothar I 817 to 855

Charles I (the Bald) 840 to 877

Louis II 855 to 875

Charles (the Fat) 884

Hugh Capet 987 to 996

Robert II (le Pieux) 996 to 1031

Henri I 1031 to 1060

Philip I 1060 to 1108

Louis VI (the Fat) 1108 to 1137

Louis VII (le Jeune) 1137 to 1180

Philip II (Augustus) 1180 to 1223

Louis VIII (the Lion) 1223 to 1226

Louis IX (St. Louis) 1226 to 1270

Philip III (le Hardi) 1270 to 1285

Philip IV (the Fair) 1285 to 1314

Louis X (le Hutin) 1314 to 1316

Philip V (the Tall) 1316 to 1322

Charles IV 1322 to 1328

Philip VI 1328 to 1350

John II 1350 to 1364

Charles V (the Wise) 1364 to 1380

Charles VI 1380 to 1422

Charles VII 1422 to 1461

NORWAY

Olaf I (Tryggvesson) 995 to 1000

Olaf II (St. Olaf) 1015 to 1028

Canute, Cnut, Cnute 1028 to 1035

Magnus I (the Good) 1035 to 1047

Harald III (Hardrada) 1047 to 1066

Magnus II 1066 to 1069

Olaf III (Kyrre) 1066 to 1093: Kyrre means "man of peace." He ruled alongside his brother until his brother's death.

Magnus III (the Barefoot) 1093 to 1103

Olaf Magnusson 1103 to 1115

Eyestein I 1103 to 1122

Sigurd 1103 to 1130

Magnus IV 1130 to 1135

Harald IV 1135 to 1136

Sigurd II 1136 to 1155

Inge I (Hunchback) 1136 to 1161

Eyestein II 1142 to 1157

Haakon II 1161 to 1162

Magnus V (Erlingsson) 1161 to 1184

Sverre (Sigurdsson) 1184 to 1202

Haakon III (Sverresson) 1202 to 1204

Inge II (Baardsson) 1204 to 1217

Haakon IV (the Old) 1217 to 1263

Magnus VI (the Law Mender) 1263 to 1280

Erik II (Magnusson) 1280 to 1299

Haakon V (Magnusson) 1299 to 1319

Magnus VII 1319 to 1355

Haakon VI 1343 to 1380

Olaf IV 1380 to 1387

Margaret 1387 to 1412: She was the mother of Olaf IV and also Queen of Denmark. Through her, the two countries were united.

WALES

Llywelyn ap Seisyll 999 to 1023

Rhydderch ab Iestyn 1023 to 1033

Iago ab Idwell 1033 to 1039

Gruffydd ap Llywelyn 1039 to 1063

Bleddyn ap Cyfyn 1063 to 1075

Trahaern ap Caradog 1075 to 1081

Gruffydd ap Cynan 1081 to 1137

IRELAND

Brian Borumha (or Boru) 1002 to 1014

Mael Sechmaill II 1014 to 1022

Turlough (Tairredelbach) O'Brien 1072 to 1086

Murtough O'Brien 1086 to 1114

Donnell O'Loughlin 1090 to 1118

Turlough O'Connor 1118 to 1156

Murtough MacLoughlin 1156 to 1166

Rory O'Connor 1166 to 1186

FOR FURTHER READING

Christopher Allmand, *Henry V.*
Maurice Ashley, *William I.*
J.W. Baldwin, *The Government of Philip Augustus.*
Richard Barber, *Henry Plantagenet 1133 to 1189.*
———— *The Devil's Crown: A History of Henry II and His Sons.*
Frank Barlow, *Edward the Confessor.*
G.W.S. Barrow, *Robert Bruce.*
———— *The Kingdom of the Scots.*
J.C. Becket, *A Short History of Ireland.*
Johannes Bronsted, *The Vikings.*
D.A. Bullough, *The Age of Charlemagne.*
F. Byre, *Irish Kings and High Kings.*
D.O. Corrain, *Ireland Before the Normans.*
R.R. Davies, *Conquest, Coexistence and Change: Wales 1063 to 1415.*
R.H.C. Davis, *King Stephen.*
T.K. Derry, *A Short History of Norway.*
R.H.M. Dolley, *Anglo-Norman Ireland.*
David C. Douglas, *William the Conqueror.*
A.A.M. Duncan, *Scotland: The Making of the Kingdom.*
Robert Fawtier, *The Capetian Kings of France.*
A. Fisher, *William Wallace.*
F.L. Ganshof, *The Carolingians and Frankish Monarchy.*
J. Gillingham, *The Life and Times of Richard I.*
R.A. Griffiths, *The Reign of Henry VI.*
Elizabeth Hallam, *Capetian France 987 to 1328.*
J.C. Holt, *King John.*
E.F. Jacob, *Henry V and the Invasion of France.*
E. James, *The Origins of France from Clovis to the Capetians.*
Gwyn Jones, *A History of the Vikings.*

W.C. Jordan, *Louis IX and the Challenge of the Crusade*.

P.M. Kendall, *Louis XI*.

S. Keynes, *The Diplomas of King Aethelred 'The Unready'*.

J.E. Lloyd, *History of Wales from the Earliest Times to the Edwardian Conquest*.

Elizabeth Longford, ed., *The Oxford Book of Royal Anecdotes*.

H.R. Loyn, *Harold Godwinson*.

J.D. Mackie, *A History of Scotland*.

Charles MacKinnon, *Scottish Highlanders*.

R. McKitterick, *The Frankish Kingdoms Under the Carolingians*.

J.L. Nelson, *Politics and Ritual in Early Medieval Europe*.

Sidney Painter, *The Reign of King John*.

Alan Palmer, *Kings and Queens of England*.

Charles Plummer, *The Life and Times of Alfred the Great*.

F.M. Powicke, *King Henry III and the Lord Edward*.

M.C. Prestwich, *The Three Edwards*.

Katharine Scherman, *Birth of France: Warriors, Bishops, and Long-Haired Kings*.

Ronald McNair Scott, *Robert the Bruce*.

A.P. Smyth, *Scandinavian Kings in the British Isles*.

Joseph R. Strayer, *The Reign of Philip the Fair*.

David Walker, *Medieval Wales*.

J.M. Wallace-Hadrill, *The Long-Haired Kings*.

Ralph Whitlock, *The Warrior Kings of Saxon England*.

M.L. Wilks, *The Problem of Sovereignty in the Later Middle Ages*.

David Williamson, *Kings and Queens of Britain*.

CHAPTER TWELVE

QUEENS

The role of queen varied greatly from country to country and from woman to woman. Some queens, such as Eleanor of Aquitaine, were heavily involved in politics and war. Others, such as Berengaria de Navarre, had next to no contact with their countries. In fact, Berengaria never stepped foot on English soil in her life. Then, there are other queens about whom we know next to nothing. For this reason, I urge writers to do extensive research when they decide to use a queen in their work.

❊ ❊ ❊

ENGLAND

Eahlswith (Elswyth): Married Alfred in 868. D. December 5, 902.

Ecgwynn (Egwina): First wife of Edward the Elder.

Elfleda: Second wife of Edward the Elder.

Eadgifu (Edgiva): Third wife of Edward the Elder.

Elfgifu (Elfgiva): First wife of Edmund I.

Ethelfleda: Second wife of Edmund I.

Elfgiva: Secret wife of Edwy the Fair. D. September 959.

Ethelfleda: First wife of Edgar the Peaceful. M. 961. D. 962.

Elfthrith (Elfrida): Second wife of Edgar the Peaceful. M. 964. D. November 17, 1000.

Elfgiva: First wife of Aethelred the Unready. M. ca. 985.

Emma (Also called Elfgiva): Second wife of Aethelred the Unready. M. 1002.

Gunhild: First wife of Sweyn Forkenbeard.

Sigrid the Haughty: Second wife of Sweyn Forkenbeard.

Ealdgith: Wife of Edmund Ironside. M. 1015.

Emma (the same Emma who had married Aethelred the Unready): Recalled to England, she married Canute on July 2, 1017. D. March 6, 1052.

Eadgyth (Edith): Wife of Edward the Confessor. M. January 23, 1045. D. December 18, 1075.

Ealdgyth: Wife of Harold Godwineson. M. 1065.

Matilda: Wife of William the Conqueror. B. ca. 1031. M. 1053. D. November 2, 1083.

Matilda of Scotland: First wife of Henry I. B. ca. 1079. M. November 11, 1100. D. May 1, 1118.

Adeliza of Loucain: Second wife of Henry I. B. ca. 1105. M. January 29, 1122. D. 1151.

Matilda of Boulogne: Wife of Stephen. B. ca. 1104. M. 1125. D. May 3, 1152.

Eleanor of Aquitaine: Wife of Henry II. B. ca. 1122. M. May 18, 1152. D. 1204.

Berengaria of Navarre: Wife of Richard the Lion Heart. B. ca. 1163. M. May 12, 1191.

Isabella of Gloucester: First wife of John. M. 1189, Divorced in 1199.

Isabella of Angouleme: Wife of John. B. ca. 1188. M. August 24, 1200. D. May 31, 1246.

Eleanor of Provence: Wife of Henry III. B. ca. 1223. M. January 14, 1236. D. June 24, 1291.

Eleanor of Castile: First wife of Edward I. B. ca. 1244. M. 1254. D. November 24, 1274.

Margaret of France: Second wife of Edward I. B. 1279. M. September 10, 1299. D. February 14, 1317.

Isabella of France: Wife of Edward II. B. 1295. M. January 25, 1308. D. August 22, 1358.

Philippa of Hainault: Wife of Edward III. B. June 24, 1311. M. January 24, 1328. D. August 14, 1369.

Anne of Bohemia: First wife of Richard II. B. May 11, 1346. M. January 1382. D. June 3, 1394.

Isabella of France: Second wife of Richard II. B. November 9, 1389. M. November 1, 1396. D. September 13, 1409.

Joan of Navarre: Wife of Henry IV. B. ca. 1370. M. September 11, 1386. D. July 9, 1437.

Catherine of France: Wife of Henry V. B. October 27, 1401. M. June 2, 1420. D. January 3, 1437.

Margaret of Anjou: Wife of Henry VI. B. March 23, 1429. M. 1445. D. August 25, 1482.

FOR FURTHER READING

Antonia Fraser, *The Warrior Queens*.
Amy Kelly, *Eleanor of Aquitaine and the Four Kings*.
Nora Lofts, *Queens of England*.
Elizabeth Longford, *Royal Anecdotes*.
John Matthews, *Boadicea*.
Desmond Seward, *Eleanor of Aquitaine: The Mother Queen*.
Graham Webster, *Boudica*.
David Williamson, *Kings and Queens of Britain*.

CHAPTER THIRTEEN

TITLES

hese are a list of English titles used after the Norman invasion, and the dates when they began to be used. Other titles are found in the sections of their countries. Many titles that we take for granted today such as Marquis, Baroness, Duchess, and such were unknown through most of the Middle Ages. Always double check the dates before using the title.

When having characters address the nobility, here is a quick list of common forms of address: King (Your Grace, Sire, Your Majesty), Queen (Your Grace, Your Majesty), Lords (milord, m'lord), Ladies (milady, m'lady), Earl's wife (Countess).

The title king or *cyning* is the oldest of the British titles. In England, it was used as the title for the Heptarchy, the rulers of England's seven kingdoms. Noblemen were styled aldermen or aeldermen, and after the Conquest this changed to baron. Alderman ranked below *eorls*. Neither of these titles were hereditary rights.

In France, titles such as viscount, count and duke were used, and after the Conquest, it was possible to have an English lord styled by one of these titles when referring to his French holdings, but not for his English possessions. However, after the Conquest, the title viscount was used for sheriffs. High Sheriff was another common title for that office.

Only the possessors of the title were rightfully styled by it. Their children were not. However, the children of land-holding barons were called lord and lady as a courtesy, and many of the elder sons and at times younger sons were given property and titles by their fathers until they came into either their own holdings or inherited their father's lands.

The wife of any nobleman, even a knight once the knight became recognized as a nobleman, was styled lady.

The order of ranking from lowest to highest was: baron, earl, duke, king. However, the term baron was deceptive. It could also include earls and dukes. But when it was the sole title, then its bearer ranked below the others.

Titles were originally granted by tenure. If the person held lands from the king, he/she was a baron. Titles were also granted by a letter of patent, charter, writ, or a summons to the Great Council which existed before parliament.

❖ ❖ ❖

OFFICES AND DATES

Banneret: A knight who led knights under his own banner.

Baron: Tenant-in-chief who held lands.

Baroness: Fourteenth-century title for the wife of a Baron.

Baronet: Fourteenth-century title used for nobles who didn't hold land, but were members of the House of Lords.

Countess: Wife of an earl.

Duchess: Fourteenth-century title used for the wife of a duke.

Duke: Given to the members of the royal family.

Earl: The highest of the nobility.

King: Ruler of England.

Knight: A soldier, not necessarily a member of the nobility.

Knight-Errant: Late fourteenth-century term for a knight who wandered in search of adventure.

Lady: General term used for noblewomen.

Prince: Son of the king.

Princess: Daughter of the king.

Queen: Wife of the king.

Sir: Mid-thirteenth century term used to designate knights.

FOR FURTHER READING

L.G. Pine, *Titles: How the King Became His Majesty.*
Selden, *Titles of Honour.*
———— *Works of Selden* (vol. 3).
Gustav Tengvik, *Old English Bynames.*

CHAPTER FOURTEEN

KNIGHTS

T hough the concept of knighthood and courtly love as we know it doesn't appear until the twelfth century, the roots that made these two possible extend far into the past. It was Charlemagne who introduced the idea of a mounted soldier and combined it with the land grant that we associate with feudalism.

In the early stages, knights were not the same as noblemen. They were servants and fighters of their overlord and held his lands for him. Upon their deaths the lands reverted automatically to the lord for him to give to whomever he pleased. The lord often granted the land to the former vassal's son. In little time, this became a birthright.

The concept of knighthood evolved during the twelfth and thirteenth centuries. It is also during this time that the rituals associated with knighting ceremonies, chivalry and courtly behavior grew up. And social ranks began to close.

Prior to the twelfth century, any man who could afford equipment and training could be knighted. After this, the birthright became increasingly important, a fact that also led to the interest in genealogy and heraldry.

Though Charlemagne, in the eighth century, and the English epic *Beowulf* speak of kings giving arms and equipment to their men, it's not until the knighting of Geoffrey of Anjou by King Henry I of England that we see the formalized knighting ceremony for the first time.

By the end of the period, the ceremonies had become so formalized and expensive that many squires couldn't afford their knighting ceremonies and remained servants their whole lives. Much like a modern debutante, the knight was expected to be suited by his father

A squire helps a knight prepare for a tournament. Here the squire ties a greave to the knight's shin.

with only the finest, most expensive and modern equipment. The father was also expected to throw a massive feast and give alms.

During the thirteenth century, the church stepped in and ritualized the ceremony. Now the squire was expected to pray and keep vigil the night before his "debut." When the blessed morning arrived, he would be bathed, clothed and armed with great care, then led to an upper-ranking nobleman who would dub him with a blow and welcome him to knighthood.

Once knighted, the knight would display his skills in a tournament. However, it is important to remember that the tournament was heavily objected to by the church. In fact, tournaments were illegal in England until Richard I issued a writ in 1194 that legalized them in five areas: Suffolk, Wiltshire, Warwickshire, Northamptonshire and Nottinghamshire.

Before the reign of Richard, standard knighting ceremonies were informal and consisted of nothing more than a dispensation of arms. The knight would journey to Normandy or the Low Countries to join the tourney circuits there. He would try to gain a name for himself as well as wealth. Many who did this also moved on to become highly paid mercenaries who hoped to gain land and title by serving a nobleman in war.

If knighted in battle, the squire would receive arms and his customary collee (a swift blow to the head). By the reign of Henry II, however, the number of knights in a household began to drop as more noblemen were paying scutage than were actually supplying men or service. This is another reason why mercenaries became so important during the second half of the twelfth century.

A knight's equipment consisted of his horse, shield, sword, hauberk, lance, saddle, bridle and helm. Most noblemen only kept seven to twenty knights on hand with twenty being a big household and very unusual.

TOURNAMENT PRIZES

Animals

Armor or pieces of armor

Capturing horses, men or armor allowed the knight who captured them to demand ransom or sell what he could.

Clothing and/or expensive cloth

Gold or silver belts

Gold-, silver- or jewel-encrusted statues or cups.

Jewelry of all sorts

Swords

❊ ❊ ❊

TOURNAMENTS

When someone thinks of knights in the Middle Ages, one of the first images that comes to mind is the tournament. Yet throughout the period, the church wrote against, banned and condemned tournaments. In fact, most clergymen refused Christian burial and last rites to anyone killed while tourneying.

Despite this condemnation by the church, tournaments were one of the most important activities any knight could partake in. In their beginning (late eleventh century), tournaments or melees were more like real war than games. Knights wore the same heavy armor they fought in and many knights died. There were also cases of knights and noblemen ganging up on their enemies and using the melee as a cover for murder.

It was during the twelfth century that rules and boundaries for

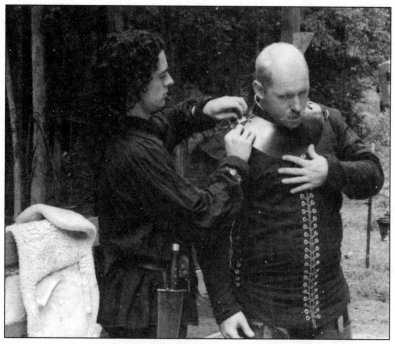

The squire clasps the gorget, which protects the knight's neck and shoulders.

tournaments first appeared. And during the thirteenth century, you begin to see lighter armor and blunted weapons designed for the new type of tournament that was evolving—a plaisance and joust. By the fifteenth century, the tournament was all pageant and spectacle.

TERMS ASSOCIATED WITH KNIGHTHOOD

A outrance: A melee tourney fought with war weapons and armor. Very few rules applied and entrants could be killed or maimed.

A plaisance: A pleasant tourney fought for show. Blunted weapons and lighter armor were used.

Bohort: A game where squires fought with blunted weapons and padded armor.

Berfrois: The stand where lady spectators sat, though other important guests were also allowed.

The squire laces the vambrace, which protects the knight's arm.

Coup de Jarnoc: A cut across the hamstring.

Course: A round of fighting, or one run of joust.

Commencailles: The first stage of a tourney where a few chosen knights showed their skills to the guests.

Estoc: A type of move in which a small, sharp estoc (knife) was driven under the opponent's ribs. This move was forbidden from games and a plaisance.

Estramacon: A sword cut.

Etoupin: A skirmish.

Feat of Arms: A game like a triathalon where knights displayed a variety of skills on both horseback and foot.

Hastilude: A game or sport that used a lance or spear.

Joust: A match fought with lances by two knights.

Melee: A dangerous form of tourney fought on horseback or foot. Few rules were used and most weapons were lethal.

The squire hoists the breastplate and backplate over the knight's head.

Peacock: A type of quintain.

Quintain: A pole that had a cross beam. A sack of sand and a shield were placed on either end of the crossbeam and a knight or squire charged it with a lance. The object was to strike the shield and get out of the way before the other arm knocked the rider from his saddle.

Rebated: Blunting weapons used for a plaisance combats.

Recet: The free zone where knights could withdraw and rest or hold prisoners.

Round Table: A celebration that revolved around the Arthurian legends.

Tenant: A knight who challenged all comers, then held the field against them.

Tilt: English word for a joust.

The squire straps the sword, scabbard and belt around the knight's waist.

Venant: One who answered a tenant's challenge.

Vespers/Vigils: A trial run for the lesser experienced combatants to practice the night before a tourney or joust.

FOR FURTHER READING

Richard Barber, *The Reign of Chivalry.*
————— *The Knight and Chivalry.*
R. Barber and J. Barker, *Tournaments: Jousts, Chivalry and Pageants in the Middle Ages.*
B.B. Broughton, *Dictionary of Medieval Knighthood and Chivalry: People, Places and Events.*
Andreas Capellanus, *The Art of Courtly Love.*
Peter Coss, *The Knight in Medieval England 1000 to 1400.*
F.H. Cripps-Day, *The History of the Tournament.*
W.S. Davis, *Life on a Medieval Barony: A Picture of a Typical Feudal Community in the Thirteenth Century.*
A.J. Denomy, *The Heresy of Courtly Love.*
Georges Duby, *The Chivalrous Society.*

The knight puts on his helm.

——————— *The Three Orders: Feudal Society Imagined.*

D. Edge and J.M. Paddock, *Arms and Armor of the Medieval Knight.*

Charles Foulkes, *The Armourer and His Craft from the XIth to the XVIth Century.*

Frances Gies, *The Knight in History.*

Christopher Gravett, *Knight.*

C. Harper-Bill and R. Harvey, *Medieval Knighthood* (4 vols).

Andrea Hopkins, *Knights.*

C.S. Jaeger, *The Origins of Courtliness: Civilizing Trends and the Formation of Courtly Ideals, 939 to 1210.*

Maurice Keen, *Chivalry.*

W.C. Meller, *A Knight's Life in the Days of Chivalry.*

A.V.B. Norman, *The Medieval Soldier.*

Francesco Rossi, *Medieval Arms and Armour.*

The fully armored knight is ready for the joust.

R. Rudorff, *Knights and the Age of Chivalry.*
W.A. Shaw, *The Knights of England* (2 vols.).

CHAPTER FIFTEEN

HERALDRY

The exact date heraldry originated is hard to pinpoint. The first evidence of its use can be found in the Bayeaux Tapestry (dated eleventh century) where King Harold Godwinson of England and Duke William of Normandy have gonfanons (lance flags) decorated with their personal emblems held by their standard bearers. We also see geometric designs painted on the Norman shields.

Also in the Bayeaux Tapestry, we see evidence that the first to bear heraldic badges were the most important players in a battle—the commanders.

In fact, it almost cost Duke William the campaign when at the Battle of Hastings his men couldn't identify him in the heat of battle and a rumor surged that the Duke was dead. In an effort to save his campaign, Duke William pulled off his helm and shouted at his soldiers to return to battle. On seeing that their commander still retained his health and head, the knights returned to win England from King Harold.

Ganfanons and banners continued to be the primary source of heraldry before the twelfth century and especially during the First Crusade. It allowed knights to identify their commanders and gave them a rallying point where they could regroup before making another attack. By the late twelfth century, the ganfanon was replaced by the banner for the higher ranking nobility.

We don't see many examples of heraldic devices used on shields or surcoats until the twelfth century, especially in the latter part when the advent of the Great Helm (which covered the knight's face) made all knights need an easy way to identify themselves to their allies and enemies.

In the beginning, there was no set order to heraldic devices and, as is often seen in drawings and seals, the shields did not always correspond to the banner, ganfanon or surcoat. Though many agree it was the knights who brought order to their arms and arms dispensation, Rodney Dennys in *The Heraldic Imagination* argues that it was the heralds, lawyers and writers who standardized the system.

Whatever the origin, heraldry as we know it began (though not in a true hereditary fashion) in the twelfth century, becoming popular in the thirteenth, and continuing to develop over the next two hundreds years during which it became a rigid science governed by rules most of which exist even today.

A banner with attired stags respectant and statant.

The first evidence of hereditary arms being dispensed is during the knighting ceremony of Geoffrey of Anjou where his future father-in-law, King Henry I of England, hung a shield—azure with lioncels—about his neck. We again see a similar shield used by Geoffrey's grandson, but again, true hereditary arms dispensations are far in the future.

It was during the early twelfth century that all men were given at their knighting ceremony a shield that displayed their first coat of arms.

Even though some families and knights began to view their coat of arms as private property as early as the thirteenth century, there is evidence of knights changing their heraldic devices well into the fourteenth century. Arguments would often arise between lords who found themselves at tourney or war with another nobleman bearing the same arms. In such cases, the court of the constable and marshal would settle the dispute.

Further heraldry developments are evidenced by King Henry II of England, King Philip II of France, and Count Philip of Flanders who decided all their knights fighting in the Third Crusade should wear a cross identifying their country. The French wore red crosses, the English white, and the Flemish green. Also, the English Parliament in 1375 decided the troops fighting in the French wars should be dressed alike.

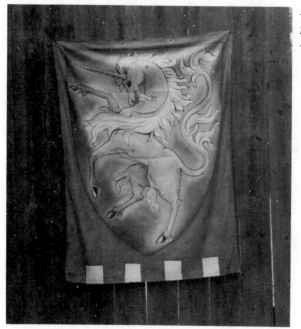

A banner with a proper unicorn statant.

In the beginning, two metals (gold and silver), five colors (red, black, blue, green and purple) and two furs (vair and ermine) were used as a base for the devices. In the fifteenth century, gems, precious stones and new colors were used as decoration for heraldic devices.

Each of the colors used was believed to have a special significance and all were referred to by their French names. Gold (or) represented the sun and was believed to be the noblest of all colors. Silver (argent) represented purity, justice and the moon. Red (gules or purpure) represented fire, boldness and virility. Green (vert), considered unlucky and worn by few, represented felicity, pleasure and youth. Blue (azure) represented justice, purity and the sky. Black (sable) represented sadness, depression and awkwardness.

The most common beasts in heraldry were the lion, the eagle and the griffin.

There were three ways to earn a coat of arms: inheritance, capture, and to be granted them.

A banner with a dragon passant.

COMMON TERMS OF HERALDRY

Achievement: The full suit of arms, including the helm, shield, surcoat and other equipment, and whatever supporters were appropriate.

Addorsed: Creatures placed back to back.

Alerion: A spread eagle that lacked a beak or feet.

Armed: Any beast on the shield whose claws, teeth or horns were a separate color from its body.

Attired: Any deer whose antlers were colored differently from its body.

Augmentation: Honors added to a crest or shield.

Banner: Used by knight-bannerets and nobles of higher rank.

Bar: A horizontal line across the shield.

Barry: Indicated there were more than three bars across a shield.

Base: The shield's bottom part.

Bend, Bendlet: A diagonal line across the shield.

Bendy: More than three bends.

Blazon: Written description of a coat of arms

Bordure: A narrow border around the field.

Caboshed: An animal's head facing forward without a neck.

Canting Arms: A pun made of the knight's name.

Charge: Name given to whatever decorated the shield.

Checky: Checks of alternating color and metal.

Chevron: A line like an upsidedown V.

Close: Wings folded against the body of a bird.

Combatant: When two charges appeared to be fighting.

Compony: When the outside border around the field was checked.

Couchant: An animal sitting or lying down with an erect head.

Counter-Changed: Two alternating field and charge colors.

Courant: The charge was running.

Cowed: A charge was subdued and usually had its tail between its legs.

Dance: A zigzag line.

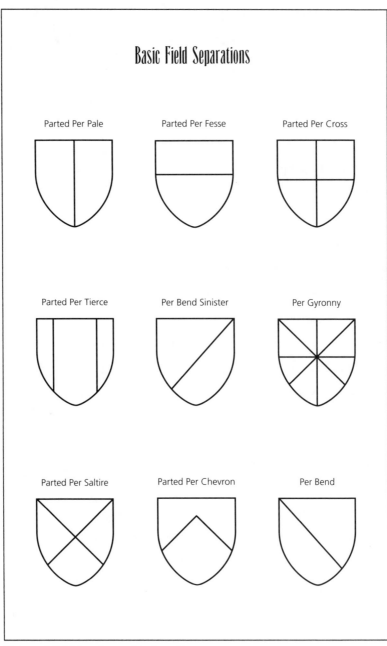

Types of field breaks used in heraldry.

Displayed: A bird with its body facing forward and its wings spread.

Erased: A charge that appeared torn apart.

Erect: Upright.

Estoile: Star.

Field: Background color.

Fitchy: The pointed bottom of a cross.

Guardant: Charge faced forward.

Lioncel: More than three lions.

Lozenge: Diamond shaped.

Membered: The legs and beak of a bird were shown.

Pale: Vertical line down the center of the shield.

Passant: The creature was walking.

Penon: Small banner used for low-ranking knights.

Proper: When the charge was its natural color.

Quarter: A quarter part in the shield.

Quatrefoil: A flower with four petals.

Rampant: A lion with its right leg raised and left foot planted. The right foot was fully raised as if to claw and the left was in a partially raised position.

Reguardant: Charge looked back over its shoulder.

Respectant: Two charges faced one another.

Salient: Charge was leaping.

Saltire: Lines formed an X over the field.

Segreant: A rampant Griffin.

Sejant: Charge was sitting.

Semee: Field covered by little charges.

Sinister: To the left.

Statant: Charge was standing.

Supporters: Characters who stood beside a coat of arms and held it.

Vested: Had clothing.

Voided: Charge was missing its center.

Volant: Charge was flying.

TIPS FOR DESIGNING A COAT OF ARMS

1. Begin with the color of the field. This is always stated first in description.
2. Choose the principle charge.
3. Choose any lesser charges that might trim or adorn the crest or shield.
4. Add the marks of distinction earned by the individual or family.

FOR FURTHER READING

R. Barber and J. Barker, *Tournaments: Jousts, Chivalry and Pageants in the Middle Ages.*

H. Bedingfeld and P. Gwynn-Jones, *Heraldry.*

J.P. Brooke-Little, *Boutell's Manual of Heraldry.*

R. Dennys, *The Heraldic Imagination.*

J. Foster, *The Dictionary of Heraldry.*

A.R. Wagner, *Heralds and Ancestors.*

———— *Heralds and Heraldry in the Middle Ages: An Inquiry into the Growth of the Armorial Functions of Heralds.*

T. Wise, *Medieval Heraldry.*

CHAPTER SIXTEEN

CASTLES

astles first appeared in Normandy during the tenth century. Though their appearance in England has often been attributed to the Norman conquest, there is evidence to show that a few were built before 1066. Some of Edward the Confessor's favored Normans had previously built strongholds as early as 1050.

Not all early castles were built of wood; some were stone and some were a combination of stone and wood. However, in the period preceding the twelfth century, the familiar motte and bailey castle was predominant, especially in England. The motte and bailey consisted of a fortified hill (either natural or man-made or a combination of the two) where a wooden or stone palisade was built. Inside the palisade was the bailey and standing dominant in the bailey was a tower.

The lord usually made his residence in the tower and as such he often made the donjon very elaborate. In records and examples as early as 1100, we see multiple chambers in these donjons that could afford the lord and lady as well as prominent guests and family their own quarters. There are also cases of the lord and his family residing outside the castle and then withdrawing to it under threat. Many nobles lived in or owned manors, lodges and homes that weren't castles at all.

Though castles were known in England prior to the Conquest, they were rare. We don't see a great interest in fortification until William's attempts to quell and dominate the natives. After this initial period of building, a decline can be noted following 1150 (one cause being Henry II's dismantling of a number of unlicensed castles at the beginning of his reign in 1154).

During the twelfth century, the donjon took on a rectangular shape. Dimensions might be 113 feet high by 70 square feet with another 12 feet added for corner turrets or towers, though some castles were smaller and some a great deal larger. Walls could vary from 12 to 21 feet thick narrowing to 10 to 17 feet at the top.

The entry level was usually reserved for the great hall where meals were served. A chapel could be placed in the basement, one of the upper floors or in the forebuilding. The two or three floors above the great hall would comprise chambers for the family and guests. According to Joseph and Frances Gies, the chimney appears around the twelfth century, and by the end of the century, "the fireplace began to be protected by a projecting hood of stone or plaster which controlled the smoke more effectively and allowed for a shallower recess."

Castles could be the center of all manner of activities including offices for the sheriff, bailey, steward, local court, or where people paid their rent or taxes.

Even though castles were important in times of peace, they were designed for war. There are many ways to capture a castle. A siege was a lengthy and costly venture, but many knights were able to breech castle walls by a variety of tricks such as crawling up the garderobe chutes or poisoning the well.

Castles were defended from the walls by bowmen, guards launching various projectiles or dumping oil and fire. Occupants were also known to launch small attacks from the postern gates.

❊ ❊ ❊

TERMS ASSOCIATED WITH CASTLES

Allure: Catwalk behind the battlement.

Arcade: Arches that were supported by columns.

Arch: Types of arches, including cusped, elliptical, flat, lancet, ogee, round and segmental.

Ashlar: Smooth stone blocks used for building.

Aumry: A cupboard to hold dishes.

Bailey: The courtyard inside the castle's walls. Usually three of them existed in larger castles.

Barbican: The outer defense area that visitors entered before reaching the main gate.

Bartizan: A corner turret that overhung.

Bastion: Corner tower that opened out at the rear.

Batter: The angle at the base of towers.

Battlement: The wall built up around the catwalk to protect soldiers.

Belvedere: A raised turret.

Berm: The area of land that separated the castle's wall from the moat.

Bow Window: A round window that jutted out like a bay window.

Buttress: A pillar that took the weight of the wall and eased the stress.

Cable Moulding: Moulding that resembled a rope.

Canopy: A hood over an altar or niche.

Cesspit: The pit where the garderobe waste was collected.

Corbel: A stone bracket.

Crenelation: The battlement.

Curtains: The walls of the castle.

Donjon: The keep.

Drawbridge: The movable bridge that was lowered over a moat or hole (not used much before the late thirteenth century).

Drum Tower: A round tower that was built into the wall.

Embrasure: An opening in the wall.

En Bosse: Uncut masonry.

Enceinte: A fortified area.

Finial: The small, decorative stone that topped the merlons.

Forebuilding: An addition to the keep that protected the entrance and stairwell.

Fosse: A ditch.

Gallery: A passageway or balcony that overlooked the great hall.

Garderobe, Garde Robe: A privy.

Glacis: A cliff that protected the castle.

Hoarding: A wooden gallery that allowed missiles to be dropped.

Inner Curtain: The inner wall that protected the inner bailey and buildings.

Keep: The main tower (a renaissance word, not medieval).

Loophole: A tiny opening from which arrows were shot.

Machicolations: The sunken area of the tooth-like ramparts.

Merlon: The solid part of the tooth-like ramparts.

Meurtriere, Murder Hole: An opening above a passageway where ambushes took place.

Motte: A mound of earth.

Oilette: A small, round opening in the base of a loophole.

Oriel: A bay window for an upper floor.

Oubliette: A tiny dungeon where prisoners were kept. It was so small that the person stood hunched over and could neither sit nor move into a comfortable position.

Outer Curtain: The outer wall that protected the outer bailey and buildings.

Palisade: The wooden fence used until a stone wall could be erected.

Pele: A Scottish defense. A small tower.

Pit prison: A prison sunk into the ground that was accessed by a trap door.

Portcullis: The grated gate that lowered to protect a doorway or gate.

Postern: A small gate.

Put-Logs: Supported a hoarding.

Quadrangle: Inner courtyard of a building.

Sally-Port: Postern gate.

Screen: Divided the kitchen from the great hall, or an area where food was taken before it was served.

Shell-Keep: The stone wall built on top of a motte.

Slight: To ruin a castle in order to keep someone else from using it.

Solar: The private chambers.

Stoup: Held holy water.

Truss: A timber frame built over the great hall that supported the roof.

Turret: A small tower usually used for lookout.

FOR FURTHER READING

W.F.D. Anderson, *Castles of Europe: From Charlemagne to the Renaissance.*

Ella Armitage, *Early Norman Castles.*

Stephen Biesty, *Incredible Cross Sections.*

R.A. Brown, *English Castles.*

———— *Castles.*

———— *The Architecture of Castles: A Visual Guide.*

Conrad Cairns, *Medieval Castles.*

James Forde-Johnston, *A Guide to the Castles of England and Wales.*

Plantagenet Somerset Fry, *The Tower of London: Cauldron of Britain's Past.*

Joseph and Frances Gies, *Life in a Medieval Castle.*

Paul Johnson, *Castles of England, Scotland and Wales.*

Maurice Lindsay, *The Castles of Scotland.*

David Macaulay, *Castle.*

Fiona MacDonald and Mark Bergin, *A Medieval Castle.*

Colin Platt, *The Castle in Medieval England and Wales.*

Sidney Toy, *Castles: Their Construction and History.*

R.J. Unstead, *A Castle.*

CHAPTER SEVENTEEN

SERVANTS

elow is a list of the types of servants a large household might employ. Some duties were performed by fostered children, others by hired servants, and still others by men and women who owed service to the lord. Those who owed service to the lord functioned in a rotating manner. If they owed him two weeks service, they would leave at the end of the period and another servant would take their place. Hired servants were often given a place to sleep inside the donjon, usually in the great hall. They obtained their jobs in much the same way we do today. After inquiring if an opening was available, they would present hand-written recommendations, provided they had them, and would interview with either the lord or with the overseer of the area in which they hoped to work.

The number of servants working in a castle depended on the wealth of the lord. In a poorer castle, jobs would be combined or omitted. A wealthy lord might employ all and might even take them along as he travelled about the land and between his own estates. Or he might fire any or all of them, then rehire more servants once he settled in his residence.

An interesting side note is that most servants were unmarried men. Many medieval guides for employment urged the head of the household to keep the number of women in a household (even if they were married) as small as possible. More times than not, unmarried men moved through the ranks and were promoted and better paid than their married counterparts. For this reason, a large number of church clerics were hired by lay employers.

But records exist of women who were employed in some of the more powerful positions, many of whom were the widows of the men who had performed those duties such as steward or butler. The majority of these women were employed by women who ran the castle and who were usually widows themselves. Some records show that the women held the position only until a suitable man could be found, but other records indicate that they maintained the position until they either choose to leave or died.

But there were certain positions reserved for women only, such as lady's maid, lady-in-waiting (who were often the social equals of the lady), laundresses, nurse or wet nurse. These women came under the direction of the woman of the household and in the event of her death (with the exception of laundresses and wet nurse for an infant) were usually released from their positions.

Due to the scarcity of female positions, many parents sought early employment for their daughters. There are also a number of cases of women who were admitted conjointly with their husbands, but in such cases it was due to the husband's desirability and was at the husband's insistence as terms for his employment.

Most guides also urged employers not to hire relatives for any position. Just as today, often relatives would take advantage of their employer, or could cause problems for the employer.

❊ ❊ ❊

Acrobat: Performed acts of agility and dexterity.

Almoner: Distributed alms.

Archer: Bowman.

Avener: Oversaw stable.

Bailiff: Oversaw manor.

Brewer/Brewster: Brewed the ale or cider.

Butler: Bought and stored supplies.

Carver: Carved the meat.

Castellan: Governed the castle.

Chamberlain: Valet in charge of the master's quarters.

Chamber Maid: Low-born attendant who cleaned.

Chandler: Made candles.

Chaplain: Monk or priest in charge of the chapel (also could perform the duties of a secretary).

Chief Cook: Oversaw the cooking and created unique recipes.

Clerk: Kept records and accounts and wrote letters.

Clerk of the Kitchen: Served meals, kept accounts of purchases and occasionally served the high table.

Cook: Prepared meals.

Crossbowman: Attended the defense of the castle.

Cupbearer: Tasted drinks for imperfections. Also kept all the cups full.

Dairy Maid: Milked cows and made cheese.

Dresser: Arranged food on serving platters.

Ewerer: Carried the ewer and washed hands.

Falconer: Attended the mews.

Foot-soldier: Low-born soldier.

Gentleman-in-Waiting: A valet.

Gentleman Usher: In charge of the door, introduced guests and oversaw the upstairs areas.

Groom: Took care of the horses and stable.

Hayward: In charge of hedges.

Henchman: Male attendant.

Herald: Messenger and a master of ceremonies.

Indoor Groom: Followed the orders of the gentleman usher.

Jester/Fool: Court comedian and philosopher.

Juggler: Juggled.

King of Arms/Leading Herald: Presented challenges at tournaments.

Kitchen Boy/Scullion: Kitchen helper and dish washer.

Kitchen Maid: Kitchen helper.

Knight: Horse soldier.

Lady's Gentlewoman/Lady-in-Waiting/Lady's maid: Attended the lady of the hall and was usually high born.

Laverer: Washed the hands of diners.

Magician: Performed magic.

Marshal: Regulated processions and ceremonies (originally in charge of the stable).

Master of Venerie: Presented the best carcasses as trophies for a hunt.

Mat Weaver: Made the mats that replaced the rushes.

Mesnie: Soldiers.

Mime: Mimes.

Minstrel: Sang songs and recited poetry.

Musician: Played an instrument.

Nursery Maid: Worked in the nursery.

Page: Made beds, helped to replace rushes, performed general errands as assigned, and sometimes doubled as the cup bearer.

Pantler: Oversaw the pantry, distributed bread and prepared trenchers.

Patisser: Made pastries and cakes.

Priest: Oversaw the spiritual necessities of the manor or castle.

Provost: Royal magistrate.

Quistron: Turned the spit.

Reeve, Sheriff: Collected taxes and upheld the laws of the shire and lord.

Rotisser: Designed and prepared roasted food.

Saucer: Made sauces, gravies and glazes.

Servitor: Served food.

Spinner: Woman who spun wool.

Squire: Oversaw his master's arms and horse.

Steward/Stewart/Surveyor/Seneschal: Oversaw the castle and demesne.

Sweeper: Swept the courtyard.

Taster: Tasted food.

Warner: Created subtleties.

Wet Nurse: Fed the babies.

Woodward: Oversaw the forest.

...prime ... la chualeo ...
... dur. bianc samt.
... uestu et aparellie se li ...
... moi sire chi. et il li fist et
... au siege pilleus. de la
... bene le diax dont il ...
... u uoit fere ... se ...
...deu a est ... fere ... al ...
...ne regarde ... la lettre ...
... le nom a ... ...
...ent. Sire chi. asen ne
... nit ... ce li fist rot ...
... apresome ... ...
... et ane fer ce ... en ...
... lua mo ... ... a ...

PART THREE

God & War

CHAPTER EIGHTEEN

THE CHURCH

O ne of the primary points to remember about the church in the Middle Ages is that its policy and power changed drastically and rapidly. There were times when the church's power was weak and other times when it was strong. Its strength was usually drawn from an alliance with a powerful lay authority, or in the words of R.W. Southern, "England . . . Germany and France — were the only places where papal influence could be strong because it was strongly desired."

The pope headed the unified church in Rome until the second schism in 1054 when the patriarch of Constantinople refused to bow to the Roman pope. Whereas the Greek and Roman church had reunified after the first schism in 867, the second one succeeded in separating the two churches forever.

The pope, unlike the patriarch who was appointed by the emperor, was elected to his office by the college of cardinals. Under the cardinals followed the archbishops (oversaw provinces), bishops (oversaw dioceses), regular clergy (friars, monks and nuns), and secular clergy (laybrothers and stewards).

Throughout the period, arguments were made and policies were changed regarding the church's authority. In fact, the reality of papal supremacy, though an idea as old as the first century, wasn't effectively claimed until the Gregorian reforms of the late eleventh century. But for all Pope Gregory VII's reforms, he still ended his life deposed and deprived of his papal throne. And even with his reforms, most of the following popes had a difficult time enforcing them.

One reason for this was that the church allowed all its punishments to be carried out by secular authority. An ecclesiastical court might find someone guilty of heresy, but they had no power to enforce the sentence. Therefore the pope and church relied on lay powers to secure punishments.

The pope's curia was the final appeal for all people called before the canon court. All of the church's members, including lay clergy, could be tried by the ecclesiastical courts rather than secular.

Everyday religious ceremonies were performed by the vicar or rector who was appointed by the diocese's bishop. It was the vicar or rector's job to perform the day-to-day ceremonies, such as burials and christenings, for the parish's people.

Celibacy was preferred from the fourth century on, but it wasn't completely enforced until the twelfth. Even after this, there are still plenty of records and letters illustrating that a number of clergy kept concubines or sought the opposite sex.

A man must be at least twenty-five years old to qualify as a priest and thirty to qualify as a bishop (originally, thirty was also the age for a priest, but it was lowered in 751). Despite this, any child over the age of seven could be conferred to minor orders and tonsured.

However, not everyone could be admitted to clerical office; women and the unbaptized were excluded. In some cases, the church allowed men with mental or physical deformities to be admitted, but they could never perform the duties of their office such as confession and baptism. Also included with the latter were soldiers, bastards, prosecutors and executioners.

A cleric was expected to be circumspect and honest at all times. The Third (1179) and Fourth (1215) Lateran Councils forbade clerics from participating in hunting, war, surgery, theater (they couldn't even attend it), commerce, or games of chance. Despite these prohibitions, there was still a number of clerics who did partake of forbidden fruits.

Because of their elevated station, clerics were given several privileges. For example, anyone who struck a cleric was excommunicated; clerics could not be condemned by a lay judge or court; could not be deprived of all their money or home by a creditor; and clerics were not to perform any lay duty that interfered with their vows.

※ ※ ※

THE POPES

Pelagius II 579-590
Gregory I 590-604
Martin I 649-655
Constantine I 708-715
Gregory II 715-731
Gregory III 731-741
Zacharias 741-752
Stephen II 752-757
Paul I 757-767
Stephen III 768-772
Hadrian I 772-795
Leo III 795-816
Stephen IV 816-817
Paschal 817-824
Gregory IV 827-844
Leo IV 847-855
Nicholas I 858-867
Hadrian II 867-872
John VIII 872-882
Hadrian III 884-885
Stephen V 885-891
Formosus 891-896
Stephen VI 896-897
John X 914-928
John XII 955-964
Benedict VI 973-974
John XIV 983-984
Gregory V 996-999
Silvester II 999-1003
John XVII 1003-1003
John XVIII 1004-1009
Sergius IV 1009-1012
Benedict IX 1012-1024
John XIX 1024-1032
Benedict IX 1032-1045
Gregory VI 1045-1046
Clement II 1046-1047
Damasus II 1047-1048
Leo IX 1048-1054

Victor II 1054-1057
Stephen IX 1057-1058
Benedict X 1058-1059
Nicholas II 1058-1061
Alexander II 1061-1073
Gregory VII 1073-1085
Victor III 1086-1087
Urban II 1088-1099
Paschal II 1099-1118
Gelasius II 1118-1119
Calixtus II 1119-1124
Honorius II 1124-1130
Innocent II 1130-1143
Celestine II 1143-1144
Lucius II 1144-1145
Eugenius III 1145-1153
Anastasius IV 1153-1154
Hadrian IV 1154-1159
Alexander III 1159-1181
Luscius III 1181-1185
Urban III 1185-1197
Gregory VIII Oct-Dec 1187
Clement III 1187-1191
Celestine III 1191-1198
Innocent III 1198-1216
Honorius III 1216-1227
Gregory IX 1227-1241
Celestine IV Oct-Nov 1241
Innocent IV 1243-1254
Alexander IV 1254-1261
Urban IV 1261-1264
Clement IV 1265-1268
Gregory X 1271-1276
Innocent V Jan.-June 1276
Hadrian V July-Aug. 1276
John XXI 1276-1277
Nicholas III 1277-1280
Martin IV 1281-1285
Honorius IV 1285-1287

Nicholas IV 1288-1292
Celestine V July-Dec. 1294
Boniface VIII 1294-1303
Benedict XI 1303-1304
Clement V 1305-1314
John XXII 1316-1334
Benedict XII 1334-1342
Clement VI 1342-1352
Innocent VI 1352-1362
Urban V 1362-1370
Gregory XI 1370-1378
Urban VI 1378-1389
Boniface IX 1389-1404

Innocent VII 1404-1406
Gregory XII 1406-1409
Alexander V 1409-1410
Martin V 1417-1431
Eugenius IV 1431-1439
Nicholas V 1447-1455
Calixtus III 1455-1458
Pius II 1458-1464
Paul II 1464-1471
Sixtus IV 1471-1484
Innocent VIII 1484-1492
Alexander VI 1492-1503

ANTI-POPES

In an attempt to keep all lay powers from interfering with papal authority, Pope Nicholas II decided in 1059 to leave the choice of pope up to the college of cardinals. Since the college was made up of differing cardinal ranks (cardinal bishops, cardinal priests, cardinal deacons) it was decided that the higher cardinals' votes would outweigh the lesser votes. But the value of each type of vote was never settled on, resulting in more interference from the lay powers.

Even the church wasn't always sure who had been voted into office. The confusion brought about a number of *anti-popes*, or men who claimed papal authority. Their actions caused a division of loyalty between the church's followers who didn't know which pope was the real one. The confusion didn't end until the Third Lateran Council, which granted equal vote to all cardinals and established a two-thirds majority be granted before a pope could attain his office.

Gregory 1012
Silvester III 1045
Honorius II 1061-1072
Clement III 1080-1100
Theodoric 1100
Albert 1102
Silvester IV 1105-1111
Gregory VIII 1118-1121
Anacletus II 1130-1138
Victor IV 1138

Victor V 1159-1164
Paschal III 1164-1168
Calixtus III 1168-1178
Innocent III 1179-1180
Nicholas V 1328-1330
Clement VII 1378-1394
Benedict XIII 1394-1409
John XXIII 1410-1415
Clement VIII 1423-1429
Felix V 1439-1449

ORDERS

Alcantara (Originally Order of St. Julian de Pereiro): Founded as a Spanish military order around 1176, they followed the Cistercian Rule, which called for a return to the simplicity and humbleness of Benedictine Rule.

Augustinian: Founded in the eleventh century, it was based on the writings of St. Augustine. It preached an ordinary life for the more secular clergy.

Austin Friars: Organized as a medicant order in 1256.

Beghards: Male counterpart to the Beguines.

Beguines: A female sect that sprang up in the early thirteenth century. They were never recognized by the church and in 1312 they were condemned by the Council of Vienne. Most of their members came from the middle class, but others could also be found in their ranks. The sisters either lived in communes or at home. They didn't take sacred vows and could leave the sisterhood to marry if they chose.

Benedictine: Founded by St. Benedict in the sixth century, the Benedictines followed his rule of strict poverty and living by their labors. The rule dictated every aspect of a monk's life—what to wear, what to eat, what to think, and how to pray.

Brethren of the Common Life: Established in the late fourteenth century in the Netherlands. The monks followed no rules, nor did they take oaths. They lived simple lives, copying manuscripts and studying.

Calatrava: Founded in 1158, their purpose was to defend Calatrava from the Almohads. They followed the Cistercian Rule. During the fifteenth century, they became politically active and were finally annexed by the crown in 1489.

Carmelite (also called White Friars): Founded in 1155 by hermits, they were a medicant order that practiced silence and fasting.

Carthusian: Founded in 1084 in France. The monks lived like hermits, but were also allowed to interact socially with other monks. Communal living was permitted for lay members who worked there.

Cistercian: Founded 1098 in Citeaux, France. Strictly followed the

Traditional garb of monks. The man on the left wears a Benedictine robe; the man on the right wears a Franciscan robe.

Benedictine Rule in its purest form. They flourished in rural areas and strove to be entirely self-sufficient.

Cluniac: Founded in Burgundy, they reformed the Benedictine Rule. Relying on lay labor, they concentrated on liturgical duties.

Conventuals: Franciscans who broke from Francis's teaching for strict poverty. They lasted until the fourteenth century.

Dominican Friars: Confirmed in 1216, they led a life of learning, preaching and poverty. Forbidden to own property, they begged for food.

Franciscan Friars: St. Francis, who had gathered a number of followers, presented his Primitive Rule to the pope in 1210. He forbade followers to touch money and they were expected to live by working for alms.

Friars of the Strict Observance: Popular in Italy, they attempted to uphold a strict vow of poverty and were reformers of the Franciscan order.

Hospitallers (Knights of St. John of Jerusalem, or of Rhodes): Founded around 1070 by Amalfian merchants as a hospital for the pilgrims, they were acknowledged as a military order in 1113. Mostly made up of Italians, they followed the Benedictine Rule and chose St. John the Baptist as their patron saint. They wore black cloaks that had a white cross on the left shoulder. Battle dress consisted of a red surcoat (battle pennon and shield) with a white cross centered front and back. Members fell into three classes: serving brothers, priests and knights. After the defeat of Acre (May 1292), they withdrew to Cyprus. In 1309, they took the Rhodes Island and gained their epitaph the Knights of Rhodes.

Humiliati: Began in the twelfth century in Lombardy. They were organized into a tri-order with celibate laity, married laity and sisters and canons in a double monastery.

Knights of the Sword: Merged with the Teutonic knights in 1230.

Order of the Dragon: Created by the King of Hungary to fight against the Turks. In time, the order became hereditary.

Order of the Knights of Santiago: Founded in 1170, they protected pilgrims who traveled to the Santiago de Compostela shrine. A military order, they didn't follow the Rule of Calatrava.

Premonstratensian Order (White Canons): Founded in 1120 at Premontre. They were reformed Augustinians who also followed some of the Cistercian habits.

Templars (Knights of the Temple or Poor Knights of Christ): Founded in 1119, they got their name from the donation of King Baldwin II (of Jerusalem) who gave them a house at the Temple of Solomon. Mostly made up of Frenchmen, they wore white cloaks with red crosses and used a white linen belt for their swords. They used a black and white beauseant as their battle ganfanon. In the beginning, they followed one commander, the *magiester Templariorum*. But during the thirteenth century, they expanded and formed three orders:

men at arms, knights and priests. In 1307, the order was relocated to France. Not long after that, the king accused them of homosexuality, idolatry and heresy, and confiscated all their French holdings. Any Templar found in France was arrested. England and Castile followed suit. Trials followed and a large number of Templars were executed. Their order was abolished March 3, 1314. Some of the survivors joined other orders.

Teutonic (Knights of the Sword): Much like the Templars, they were founded to serve the sick and pilgrims in the Holy Land around 1198. Mostly made up of Germans, they wore white cloaks with black crosses. They fought throughout Germany, the Baltic, Prussia and Holland to convert pagans to Christianity.

HERETICAL GROUPS

Adoptionist: Debated throughout the Middle Ages, it was their belief that God adopted Christ as his son and that Christ was a true man, not a man-God. Though condemned by a number of councils, it still persisted.

Albigenses: A segment of the Cathar movement, it began in southern France around 1144. The group grew fast and in 1167, it even held a council of its own. The assassination of legate Peter of Castelbnau in 1208 set off the papal-led crusade against them. In 1244 at Montsegur they were massacred. What few survived, moved underground.

Arianism: Followed the teachings of Arius who held that Jesus was not created from the same substance as God. Arianism appealed to a number of Christians, but was condemned by the Council of Nicaea in 325.

Bogomils: Began in the mid-tenth century. Like the gnostics, they believed in two Gods: an evil God who had created the earth and a good God who created the soul. They mostly flourished in eastern Europe in Bosnia, Bulgaria, Province and Asia Minor.

Brethren of the Free Spirit: Began in the thirteenth century in the Netherlands, Swabia and the Rhineland. Their doctrine combined Christian belief with Aristotle and exerted that the human will was supreme.

Cathars: Founded in the early eleventh century. They renounced the world, including eating meat, engaging in sex, and performing any secular activities.

Hussites: Wanted to restore communion in both bread and wine. They wanted reform in the church.

Manicheanism: An early heresy that influenced many of the later heretical beliefs. They believed that salvation could only be achieved by rejecting the body. They viewed all things that were matter as darkness or evil.

Nestorianism: Asserted that Christ possessed two natures that were not combined into one personality. Also asserted that Mary could not be the Mother of God since she only birthed the human aspect, not the divine.

Waldensians: Founded about 1176, they were to combat Catharism, but their preachers began attacking the pope and the hierarchy of the church.

TIME TABLE

312	Constantine issues the Edict of Toleration that declared Christianity was a viable religion.
313	Edict of Milan.
	Asserted toleration of both pagans and Christians.
319	Arianism begins.
320	Council of Neocaesarea
	Claimed any higher clergy who married after accepting office should be deposed.
325	Council of Nicaea.
	Asserted the Holy Trinity, the Passion, Resurrection and Incarnation of Christ. It also established the date of Easter, the first Sunday following the first full moon after the vernal equinox. Condemned Arianism.
335	Council of Tyre.
	Banished Anathasius.
358	Council of Ancyra.
	Asserted the celibacy of deacons.
359	Macedonianism begins.
362	Apollinarianism begins.
381	Second Ecumenical Council.
	Established the Nicean Creed and further defined the Trinity.

411   Augustine writes *City of God*.
429   Nestorianism begins.
430   Celestine's Council at Rome.
431   Third Ecumenical Council.
        Asserted the two natures of Christ and condemned Nestorianism.
432   Patrick journeys to Ireland.
448   Eutychianism begins.
451   Fourth Ecumenical Council (or Council of Chalcedon).
        Adopted Leo I's ideas for church reform. It also reasserted that Christ was one being possessed by two natures. It also affirmed the Roman pope as the church leader and the Byzantine patriarchate as the second in command. Monophysitism was condemned and it approved the Niceaen Creed.
484   East and West Church reconcile the first schism.
495   Gelasian Doctrine.
        A controversial document that tried to set up the roles of lay and clerical responsibilities in government. The loose wording used by Gelasius I caused a variety of interpretations—that the church should rule, that the king should have supreme power, and that it should be shared equally between them.
500   Incense is first used in church services.
511   Council of Orleans.
        Set up the church's relationship with the Frankish king.
524   Boethius is executed.
543   Origen's writings are condemned by Justinian.
550   Wales converts to Christianity.
553   Fifth Ecumenical Council.
        Asserted the two natures of Christ and denounced Nestorians who denied this. Also condemned Monophysitism.
555   Justinian claims emperor's right to confirm pope.
563   Columba begins converting Picts.
587   Visigoths converted to Christianity.
610   Episcopal rings appear.
616   Monothelism rises.
625   Mohammad begins the Qur'an.
628   Mohammad explains the basis of Muslim faith.
649   First Lateran Council.
        Condemns Monothelitism.

664   Synod of Whitby.
        Brought the Celtic Church under Roman influence.
680   Sixth Ecumenical Council.
        Asserted the two wills of Christ and denounced the Mono-
            theilites.
686   The last of England (Sussex) is converted to Christianity.
692   Quinisext Council.
        Sets up the Canon for the Eastern Church (Byzantium).
695   Jews persecuted in Spain.
697   Northern Ireland recognizes Roman Church authority.
700   Psalms are translated into Old English (Anglo-Saxon).
753   Synod of Heiria.
        Again condemned the icons.
772   Pope Adrian requests Charlemagne's aid against the Lom-
            bards.
787   Seventh Council of Nicaea.
        Regulated the icon controversy. Defended the icons.
794   Synod of Frankfurt.
        Image worship condemned. Also added the Filioque into
            the Creed. Led by Charlemagne, this set up the Theo-
            cratic monarchies that remained typical until the twelfth
            century.
842   Images were reinstated.
869   Eighth Council of Constantinople.
        Prohibited lay interference with the election of church of-
            fice.
1022   Synod of Pavia.
        Requires higher clergy to remain celibate.
1022   First heretics were burned at Orleans.
1046   Synod of Sutri.
        Called to deal with the three popes. They were deposed for
            Clement II.
1049   Council of Rheims.
        Attempted papal reform. Condemned simony, investiture,
            clerical marriage, and fees for burials.
1059   Council of Melfi.
        A defiance of the lay powers, it was summoned to combat
            the Norman threat to papal lands and to decrease the
            church's dependency on lay authority.
1059   Pope Nicholas stated that papal elections would be carried
            out by the cardinals alone.

1074   Began the excommunication of married priests.

1076   Synod of Worms.
Prohibited investiture. Pope Gregory VII excommunicated
Henry IV.

1095   Council of Clermont.
Urban II sought fighters for the First Crusade.

1121   Synod of Soissons.
Condemned Abelard's version of the trinity.

1122   Concordat of Worms.
Settled investiture.

1123   First Lateran Council.
Cracks down on simony and priest marriage. Also condemned investiture.

1139   Second Lateran Council.
Ended the schism with Byzantium.

c. 1140 Decretum of Gratian.
Developed the idea of marriage as being both a holy affair
and a state affair. Also introduced the idea that marriages
must be consummated to be valid and that the marriage's
consummation makes it a sacrament that cannot be broken. Gave guidelines for interpreting canons, it also condemned religious sects who said marriage was unfit for
Christians and that married people could not be re-
deemed.

1152   Synod of Kells.
Divided Ireland into thirty-six bishoprics and four archbish-
oprics.

1166   Assize of Clarendon.
Ordered the building of jails in England.

1170   Alexander III sets down the rules for canonization.

1173   Waldesians movement begins.

1179   Third Lateran Council.
Forbade the Humiliati to preach.

1182   All Jews were banned from France.

1184   *Ab Abolendam* was issued requiring all bishops to search their
sees for heretics and for the authorities who refused to
punish known heretics. Also denounced the Humiliati.

1185   Templars establish a base in London.

1215   Fourth Lateran Council.
Prohibited trial by ordeal. Also said no more religious orders could be formed. Stipulated that all Christians must

confess at least once a year (three times for Englishmen) and that they must confess to their local parish priests. A confession given to anyone else without the local priest's permission was invalid.

1222   Council of Oxford.
      Granted April 23 as the legal holiday for St. George.

1252   Inquisition implements torture against heretics.

1260   Flagellant movements begin in Italy and Germany.

1274   Council of Lyons.
      Attempted to unite the Roman and Greek Orthodox Churches.

1306   Jews are banned again from France.

1311   Council of Vienne.
      Condemned the Templars.

1349   Jews persecuted in Germany.

1409   Council of Pisa.
      Attempted to rectify the schism by deposing Popes Gregory XII and Benedict XIII and electing Pope Alexander V. It failed.

1414   Council of Constance.
      Tried to rectify the Great Schism. It also deposed the anti-popes: Gregory XII, John XXIII and Benedict XIII. Attempted reforms, including saying that the church's council was superior to the pope.

1431   Council of Basle.
      Tried to reform the church and to deal with the heresy of Hus's followers.

1438   Council of Florence.
      Attempted to unite Christianity. Reasserted that the pope was above his councils. The Greeks offered unification in exchange for military aid from the West. This was agreed to, but the crusade never came into being.

1484   *Summis Desiderantes* is written condemning sorcery and witchcraft.

FOR FURTHER READING

Christianity/Church

B.S. Bachrach, *Early Medieval Jewish Policy in Western Europe.*
Summerfield Baldwin, *The Organization of Medieval Christianity.*
Geoffrey Barraclough, *The Medieval Papacy.*

R.H. Bainton, *The Medieval Church.*

Bede, *A History of the English Church and People.*

John Boswell, *Christianity, Social Tolerance, and Homosexuality.*

E.G. Bowen, *Saints, Seaways and Settlements in the Celtic Lands.*

M.F. Braswell, *The Medieval Sinner.*

C.N.L. Brooke, *The Monastic World 1000 to 1300.*

R.B. Brooke, *The Coming of the Friars.*

J.A. Brundage, *Law, Sex, and Christian Society in Medieval Europe.*

Lionel Butler and Chris Given-Wilson, *Medieval Monasteries of Great Britain.*

C.W. Bynum, *Holy Feast and Holy Fast: The Religious Significance of Food to Medieval Women.*

Florens Deuchler, *Gothic.*

J.C. Dickinson, *Monastic Life in Medieval England.*

Tim Dowley, *The History of Christianity.*

W.P. Du Bose, *The Ecumenical Councils.*

Georges Duby, *The Age of Cathedrals.*

Robin Lane Fox, *Pagans and Christians.*

J.G. Frazer, *The Golden Bough.*

Hans Hollander, *Early Medieval.*

J.M. Hussey, *The Orthodox Church in the Byzantine Empire.*

Paul Johnson, *A History of Christianity.*

N.D. Kelly, *Early Christian Creeds.*

D. Knowles, *The Monastic Orders in England.*

————— *The English Mystical Tradition.*

C.H. Lawrence, *Medieval Monasticism.*

Colleen McDannell and Bernhard Lang, *Heaven: A History.*

J. Parkes, *The Jew in the Medieval Community.*

Jaroslav Pelikan, *The Spirit of Eastern Christendom (600 to 1700).*

————— *The Emergence of the Catholic Tradition (100 to 600).*

————— *The Growth of Medieval Theology (600 to 1300).*

————— *Reformation of Church and Dogma (1300 to 1700).*

————— *Jesus Through the Centuries.*

Colin Platt, *The Abbeys and Priories of Medieval England.*

J.M. Powell, *Innocent III: Vicar of Christ or Lord of the World?.*

E.K. Rand, *Founders of the Middle Ages.*

I.S. Robinson, *Authority and Resistance in the Investiture Contest.*

L.M. Smith, *Cluny in the Eleventh and Twelfth Centuries.*

R.W. Southern, *Western Society and the Church in the Middle Ages.*

F.S. Taylor, *The Alchemists.*

E.M. Thompson, *The Carthusian Order in England.*

A.R. Vine, *The Nestorian Churches*.
Alan Watts, *Myth and Ritual in Christianity*.
Schafer Williams, *The Gregorian Epoch: Reformation, Revolution, Reaction?*.
George Zarnecki, *Romanesque*.

Important Medieval Writings and Authors
St. Augustine, *City of God*.
Thomas a Kempis, *The Imitation of Christ*.
Bede, *A History of the English Church and People*.
Raphael Brown, *The Little Flowers of St. Francis*.
F.C. Copleston, *Aquinas*.
The Letters of Abelard and Heloise.
Prayers and Meditations of Saint Anselm.
Maurice Wiles and Mark Santer, eds., *Documents in Early Christian Thought*.

Heresy/Witchcraft
David Christie-Murray, *A History of Heresy*.
E.G. De Givry, *Sorcery, Magic and Alchemy*.
J.M. Klassen, *The Nobility and the Making of the Hussite Revolution*.
M.D. Lambert, *Medieval Heresy*.
Jules Michelet, *Satanism and Witchcraft*.
R.I. Moore, *The Origins of European Dissent*.
E. Peters, *Heresy and Authority in Medieval Europe*.
Jeffrey Burton Russell, *Witchcraft in the Middle Ages*.
Joseph R. Strayer, *The Albigensian Crusades*.

Military Orders
Charles G. Addison, *The History of the Knights Templar*.
Richard Barber, *The Knight and Chivalry*.
George Beltz, *Memorials of the Most Noble Order of the Garter*.
Edward Burman, *The Templars: Knights of God*.
Edwin J. King, *The Knights Hospitallers in the Holy Land*
J.H. Lawrence-Archer, *The Orders of Chivalry*.
J.F. O'Callaghan, *The Spanish Military Order of Calatrava and Its Affiliates: Collected Studies*.
Peter Partner, *The Knights Templar and Their Myth*.
E. Simon, *The Piebald Standard: A Biography of the Knights Templar*.
F.C. Woodhouse, *The Military Religious Orders of the Middle Ages*.

CHAPTER NINETEEN

SAINTS

Throughout the medieval period, saints held a special relationship with the laity and clergy. Due to their piety, faith and sacrifice, saints were viewed as having a closer relationship with God than did normal men. As such, their physical remains and presence were eagerly sought by medieval pilgrims.

Despite the criticism from the Roman Church, pagans and others, the early Christians of the East continued to disinter their dead saints and break up their bodies to use as relics. This habit didn't catch on in the West until the middle of the fourth century. From then on, the majority of popes didn't care for the practice, but they didn't take any further actions to stop it until the Fourth Lateran Council of 1215, which forbade the selling of relics. The practice, however, continued.

In fact, the popes and clergy began to find reasons why the relics of saints should be revered. Thomas Aquinas of the thirteenth century came up with three reasons:

1. Their remains and brandea (personal objects such as clothing, blood and hair) remind us of their faith and good deeds — of lives we should struggle to imitate.
2. Their bodies, having once contained such purified, blessed souls, are intrinsically good and are there to help fellow Christians.
3. God's approval of relics and pilgrims was proven by the mere fact that the remains could perform His miracles and cure the sick and needy.

Coveted by church and laity, these relics were a major commodity. One church stole from another in order to have the best relics that would guarantee them the largest number of pilgrims and thus the biggest profit. Many times, more than one church would claim to have the same relic—an embarrassment to the pope and others and a fact that gave critics a lot of fodder for their attacks.

Besides the clerics, lay collectors were also a nuisance, paying top dollar to thieves who added to their personal collections. These collectors took objects to the tombs and either touched the saint's remains, or placed their object (a piece of clothing or a handkerchief) on the saint's tomb while they prayed for the saint's goodness and healing power to transfer to their object so they could take it home and receive further benediction. The pilgrims' incessant demand for souvenirs also forced them to steal dust, break off pieces of the tomb or body, and even kiss an object so they could then bite off a piece to take home with them.

To protect their relics, lay folk often had small reliquaries made into necklaces or rings. Churches had larger reliquaries designed. The Fourth Lateran Council forbade any church to display its relics without putting them into a reliquary. From that point on, they were not to be removed from the case. In southern France during the tenth century, they began building statue reliquaries. This habit also caught on in England and Germany, but the fad died out by the twelfth century.

Yet not all relics were stolen. Hawkers lined the roadways, towns and cities offering their wares to any who could afford them. Many of these were fakes—pig bones, corpse's teeth, stray pieces of wood, blood from anything. Few of these hawkers had credentials and even fewer knew or were willing to tell the origin of their wares (another reason why collectors sought out the older, more established relics by theft).

Despite danger, pilgrims marked the highways of Europe and the Middle East in search of self and salvation. And all along their routes, charlatans and frauds abounded, each one only interested in separating the pilgrims from their purses. These dangers led to the formation of motley groups joining together to take pilgrimage in the manner of Chaucer's *Canterbury Tales.*

One interesting side effect of pilgrimages was the invention of eye glasses. During the thirteenth century, a new belief that witnesses must view the relic to receive the full benefit from it led reliquary makers to develop a very clear glass. This clear glass was used to manufacture the first pair of glasses in 1285. Over the next fifteen years, convex glasses were mass produced in Italy, and 150 years

Mid-twelfth century travelers. Their attire would have been typical for pilgrims of that time.

later, glasses were used for astigmatisms as well.

No matter how poor, all Christians did their best to buy at least one relic. Summoners, pardoners and others became rich selling relics, very few of which were ever authentic. One test for authenticity was throwing the relic into a fire or brazier. If it lasted and wasn't consumed or damaged by the flame, it was considered authentic.

❀ ❀ ❀

PILGRIMAGES

Voluntary pilgrimages were undertaken for three main reasons:

1. To grow closer to Christ and his purity by mimicing his life of wandering.
2. To gain the benediction and healing of relics (saints).
3. To atone for sins.

As an interesting side note, historian Jonathan Sumption claims

A fourteenth-century traveler. His attire would have been typical for a pilgrim of that time.

Rear view of fourteenth-century traveler. Note that he wears a dagger behind his back as well as a sword. Pilgrims frequently were set upon by thieves.

that a primary reason for pilgrimage was the penitent's desire to confess away from home and to relieve himself of the "moral censor" of his neighbors. This theory is more than plausible given the medieval belief that people should be watched and censored by their neighbors. Moreover, the Fourth Lateran Council decreed that one must confess in his or her parish, or gain the priest's consent to confess elsewhere.

I believe that another reason for pilgrimages was that many pilgrims were just medieval sightseers who wanted to travel. In addition, a number of historians further argue that pilgrimages offered an individual an escape from a dismal or painful home life.

And there is yet another reason: the penitential pilgrimage. In the sixth century, the church began prescribing pilgrimages in the Irish penitential, but this type of "punishment" quickly caught on with the rest of the Western Church. Possible sins that warranted a pilgrimage were sacrilege, murder, incest and bestiality.

In the most extreme cases, criminals were punished with eternal pilgrimages. They traveled in chains from holy site to holy site in a hopeful attempt to gain the pity and forgiveness of some saint who would break their chains and set them free. When this happened, the pilgrim would leave his chains at the shrine and was then free to live out his life.

For those who went on a voluntary pilgrimage, a number of guidebooks were drawn up, including *Liber Sancti Jacobi (Codex Calixtinus)*, which dates around 1139, and *Guide for Pilgrims to Saint James*.

As the Middle Ages progressed and the church became poorer, penitents began either paying a substitute to take the pilgrimage for them or buying indulgences. Others bought off the church once they reached the shrine, and still others participated in wars or crusades after the pope guaranteed them eternal absolution in exchange for their fighting.

Needless to say, this wasn't received well by the more religious orders or leaders. Many people feared that with so many criminals being punished this way, the roads were no longer safe. This fear led to the establishment of the hospitallers who watched over and protected religious travelers.

Despite critics, pilgrimages, for whatever reason, continued to be popular throughout the period. In the eloquent words of Jonathan Sumption, "Popular religious practices continually influence the behaviour of the establish." Indeed in many examples we find proof of his words, that in fact, the medieval Church had no choice other than to give into the demand of the lay people and allow them the pilgrimages they desired.

SAINTS AND CELEBRATION DATES

January

2 Basil (329-379)

2 Gregory of Nazianzen (329-389)

3 Genevieve (ca. 422-512, patron saint of Paris)

5 Simeon the Stylite (390-459)

7 Raymond (1175-1275)

9 Adrian of Canterbury (d. ca. 709)

10 Paul (d. 342)

11 Theodosius the Cenobiarch (423-529)

12 Benedict (d. 690)

13 Hilary (d. 368)

14 Felix of Nola (d. 260)

14 Kentigern (ca. 516-601)

15 Ita (d. ca. 570)

16 Honoratus (d. 429)

17 Antony (251-356, patron saint of monks and basketweavers)

19 Canutus (d. 1086)

20 Fabian (d. 250)

20 Sebastian (d. 288, patron saint of archers)

21 Agnes (d. ca. 305, patron saint of purity)

23 John the Almoner (d. ca. 691, patron saint of Alexandria)

26 Eystein (d. 1188)

26 Margaret (1243-1271)

26 Alberic (d. 1109)

26 Paula (d. 404, patron saint of widows)

27 Angela Merici (1475-1540)

28 Thomas Aquinas (1226-1274, patron saint of students)

29 Gildas the Wise (d. ca. 576)

February

2 Bridgit, Bride (d. ca. 525, patron saint of Ireland and dairymaids)

3 Blase, Blaise (d. 316, patron saint of throat problems)

4 Andrew Corsini (1302-1373)

4 Gilbert of Sempringham (ca. 1083-1189, patron saint of cripples)

5 Agatha (d. 251)

6 Dorothy (ca. 313)

9 Apollonia (d. 249, patron saint of tooth disorders and dentists)

10 Scholastica (d. ca. 543, patron saint of nuns)

11 Benedict of Anian (c. 750-821)

13 Ermengild (d. ca. 700)

14 Cyril and Methodius (ninth century)

14 Valentine (third century, patron saint of lovers)
15 Sigfrid of Sweden (d. ca. 1002)
16 Onesimus (d. first century)
18 Simeon, Simon (d. ca. 106)
19 Conrad (1290-1351)
20 Wulfric (d. 1154)
21 Peter Damian (ca. 988-1072)

22 Margaret of Cortona (d. 1297)
23 Polycarp (d. 166)
24 Pretextatus (d. sixth century)
25 Ethelbert (d. 616)
25 Walburgha (d. 779)
26 Porphyrius (ca. 353-420)
28 Oswald (d. 992)
29 Cassian (ca. 360-433)

March

1 David (d. 544, patron saint of Wales)
2 Ceada, Chad (d. 673)
3 Cunegundes, Kunegunde (d. 1040)
3 Winwaloe (sixth century)
4 Casimir (1310-1370, patron saint of Poland)
6 Colette (1380-1447)
7 Perpetua and Felicitas (d. 203)
9 Frances (1384-1440)
9 Gregory of Nyssa (ca. 330-395)
11 Sophronius (seventh century)
12 Maximilian (d. 295)
12 Theophanes (d. 818)
13 Euphrasia (380-410)
14 Maud, Mathildis (d. 968)
15 Zacharias (d. 752)
16 Abraham (d. ca. 360)

17 Joseph of Arimathea (first century, Patron saint of undertakers)
17 Patrick (d. 464)
18 Cyril (b. ca. 315-386)
18 Edward the Martyr (ca. 962-979)
19 Joseph (first century, patron saint of carpenters and fathers)
20 Cuthbert (d. 687, patron saint of shepherds)
22 Basil of Ancyra (d. 362)
26 Ludger (b. d. 743-809)
28 Tutilo (d. ca. 915)
29 Rupert (d. ca. 710)
30 John Climacus (b. ca. 525-605)
30 Zosimus of Syracuse (d. ca. 660)

April

1 Hugh (1053-1132)
2 Mary of Egypt (ca. 355-431)
3 Agape, Irene and Chione (d. 304)
3 Richard (1197-1253)
4 Isidore of Seville (d. 636)

5 Vincent (1357-1419)
6 William of Eskill (ca. 1125-1203)
9 Waldetrudis, Waudru (seventh century)

10 Fulbert (d. 1029)
11 Guthlac (ca. 673-714)
11 Stanislas (1030-1079)
12 Zeno (d. 380)
13 Hermenegild (d. 186)
16 Magnus of Orkney (1075-1116)
17 Stephen (d. 1134)
19 Elphege (953-1012)
20 Agnes of Montpulciano (1274-1317)
21 Anselm (b. ca. 1033-1109)
21 Beuno (sixth century, patron saint of sick animals)

22 Theodore of Sykeon (d. 613)
23 George (ca. 303, patron saint of soldiers)
24 Mellitus (d. 624)
25 Mark (ca. first century)
26 Stephen of Perm (1345-1386, patron saint of servants and wives)
27 Zita (1212-1272)
29 Catharine of Siena (1347-1380)
29 Hugh of Cluny (1024-1109)

May

1 Sigismund of Burgundy (sixth century)
2 Athanasius (b. ca. 296-373)
3 Philip (first century)
3 James the Less (d. 62)
5 Hilary (ca. 401-459)
6 Petronax (d. ca. 747)
7 John of Beverley (d. 721)
8 Peter (d. 1174)
9 Pachomius (ca. 292-348)
10 Antoninus (1389-1459)
11 Walter of l'Esterp (d. 1070)
13 John the Silent (ca. 482-559)
14 Matthias (first century)
15 Dympna (seventh century patron saint of epileptics and mental illness)
15 Isidore the Farmer (ca. 1110-1170, patron saint of Madrid and of laborers)
16 Carantoc (ca. seventh century)

16 John Nepomucen (ca. 1330-1383, patron saint of confessors)
17 Madern (sixth century)
18 Eric (d. 1151)
19 Dunstan (909-988, patron saint of the blind and goldsmiths)
20 Bernardin of Siena (1380-1444)
21 Godric (ca. 1069-1170)
22 Rita of Cascia (1377-1447)
23 Julia (fifth century)
24 David of Scotland (ca. 1085-1153)
24 Vincent of Lerins (d. ca. 450)
25 Bede (673-735, patron saint of scholars)
25 Gregory VII, Hildebrand (ca. 1021-1085)
27 Augustine (d. 604)
28 Germanus (ca. 378-448)

29 Theodosia (ninth century)

30 Ferdinand III (1199-1252, patron saint of engineers)

30 Hubert (d. 727, patron saint of hunters)

31 Mechtildis (d. 1160)

June

1 Justin (d. 167)

1 Wistan (d. 850)

2 Erasmus (d. ca. 300, patron of sailors)

3 Clotildis (d. 545)

4 Optatus (fourth century)

4 Petroc (sixth century)

5 Boniface (ca. 690-755)

6 Norbert (1080-1134)

8 William (d. 1154)

9 Columba (521-597, patron saint of poets)

9 Ephraem (d. ca. 373)

11 Barnabas (first century)

13 Antony of Padua (1195-1231, patron saint of barren women)

15 Vitus (fourth century, patron saint of nervous disorders)

16 Cyr or Quiricus (d. 304)

16 Julitta (d. 304)

17 Botulf (d. 680)

19 Juliana Falconieri (1270-1340)

19 Romuald of Ravenna (ca. 950-1027)

20 Alban (third century)

22 Paulinus of Nola (d. 431)

23 Aetheldreda, Audry (d. 679)

24 John the Baptist (d. ca. 30, patron saint of monks)

25 William of Vercelli (1085-1142)

26 Anthelm (1107-1178)

27 Cyril (d. 444, patron saint of Alexandria)

28 Irenaeus (d. 202)

29 Martha (first century, patron saint of cooks)

29 Peter (d. ca. 64, patron saint of popes and fishermen)

30 Paul (first century)

July

1 Shenute (ca. 450)

2 Otto (d. 1139)

3 Thomas (first century)

4 Elizabeth (1271-1336)

6 Godelva (d. 1070)

6 Sexburga (679-700)

7 Ethelberga (d. 665)

7 Palladius (d. ca. 450)

7 Willibald (d. 786)

8 Edgar (943-975)

8 Withburge (d. 743)

10 Secunda and Rufina (third and fourth centuries)

11 Benedict (ca. 480-543, patron saint of Western monks)

11 Thurketyl (tenth century)

12 John Gaulbert (999-1073)

12 Veronica (first century)

13 Henry the Pious (972-1024, canonized 1204, patron saint of kings)

14 Deusdedit (d. 664)

15 Bonaventure (1221-1274)
15 Swithin, Swithun (d. 862, patron saint of Winchester)
15 Vladimir (995-1015)
17 Alexis (d. 417)
17 Kenelm (d. ca. 815)
18 Elizabeth of Schonau (d. 1164)
18 Pambo of Nitria (315-385)
19 Arsenius (d. 449)
19 Macrina the Younger (ca. 327-379)
20 Vulmar (d. ca. 700)
22 Mary Magdalen (first century, patron saint of penitents)
23 Birgit, Bridget (1302-1373)
24 Christina the Astonishing (1150-1224)
24 Lupus (427-479)

25 Christopher (third century, patron saint of travelers)
25 James the Great (first century, patron saint of pilgrims)
26 Anne, Mother of Mary (first century B.C., patron saint of housewives and cabinet-makers)
27 Pantaleon (d. 303, patron saint of midwives)
28 Samson (d. 565)
29 Martha (first century)
29 Olaf (995-1030)
30 Abdon and Sennen (d. ca. 303)
30 Peter Chrysologus (d. ca. 450)
31 Germanus of Auxerre (d. 446)
31 Neot (d. ca. 877)

August

1 Ethelwold (ca. 912-984)
2 Eusebius (d. ca. 371)
2 Stephen (d. 257)
3 Waltheof (d. ca. 1160)
6 Sixtus (d. 258)
8 Dominic (1170-1221, patron saint of astronomers)
9 Oswald (604-642)
10 Laurence (d. 258, patron saint of cooks)
11 Susanna (d. ca. 295)
12 Clare (1193-1253)
13 Hippolytus (d. ca. 252, patron saint of horses)
13 Radegund (518-587)
16 Roch (1350-1380)
16 Stephen of Hungary (977-1038)
17 Hyacinth (1185-1257)

17 Clare of Montefalco (d. 1308)
18 Helen (d. ca. 326)
20 Bernard (1091-1153)
20 Oswin (d. 651)
22 Symphorianus (d. ca. 200)
23 Philip Beniti (1233-1285)
24 Bartholomew (first century, patron saint of plasterers)
24 Ouen (ca. 600-684)
25 Ebbe (d. 683)
25 Louis (1215-1270)
26 Zephryinus (d. 217)
27 Caesarius (ca. 470-542)
27 Monica (332-387, patron saint of wives)
28 Augustine (354-430, patron of theologians)
30 Fergus (eighth century)
31 Aidan (d. 651)

September

1 Drithelm (d. ca. 700)
1 Giles (seventh century, patron saint of lepers and influenza)
2 William of Roskilde (d. ca. 1070)
3 Gregory the Great (ca. 540-604, patron saint of musicians)
4 Rose of Viterbo (d. 1252)
5 Lawrence Justinian (1380-1455)
6 Bega (seventh century)
7 Cloud (ca. 522-560)
7 Sozon (fourth century)
10 Nicholas of Tolentino (ca. 1245-1306)
12 Guy of Anderlecht (d. ca. 1012)
13 John Chrysostom (d. 407, patron saint of public speakers)
14 Notburga (d. ca. 1313)
15 Adam of Caithness (thirteenth century)
16 Cornelius (d. 253)

16 Ninian (d. 432)
16 Cyprian (200-258)
17 Hildegard of Bingen (1098-1179)
17 Lambert (d. 709)
19 Januarius (d. ca. 305)
19 Theodore of Canterbury (d. 690)
20 Eustace (second century, patron saint of hunters)
21 Matthew (first century, patron saint of bankers)
22 Maurice (d. 226)
23 Adamnan (ca. 624-704)
23 Thecla, Thekla (first century)
24 Gerard (d. 1046)
25 Albert of Jerusalem (d. 1214)
26 Cosmas and Damian (ca. 303, patron saints of surgeons)
27 Sigebert (d. 635)
28 Lioba (d. 782)
28 Wenceslas (d. 938)
29 Archangels Gabriel and Michael
30 Jerome (d. 420)

October

1 Bavo (d. 633)
2 Leger (ca. 616-679)
2 Thomas of Hereford (1218-1282)
4 Francis of Assisi (1181-1226, patron saint of animals)
5 Maurus (d. 584)
6 Bruno (ca. 1030-1101)
6 Faith (third century)

7 Osith (ca. 870)
9 Dionysius, Denys (d. ca. 272)
10 Gereon (d. ca. 304)
10 Paulinus of York (d. 644)
12 Edwin (584-633)
12 Wilfrid (ca. 634-709)
13 Edward the Confessor (1002-1066)
14 Calixtus, Callistus (d. 222)

16 Hedwiges (d. 1243)
16 Gall (d. ca. 630)
17 Ignatius (d. 107)
18 Luke (first century, patron saint of physicians and painters)
19 Frideswide (ca. 680-735)
20 Acca (d. 740)
21 Hilarion (ca. 291-371)
21 Ursula (fourth century, patron saint of girls)
22 Donatus (d. 876)
23 John of Capistrano (1386-1456, patron saint of lawyers and judges)
23 Severinus Boethius (ca. 480-524)
24 Senoch (sixth century)
25 Crispin (d. 287, patron saint of tanners)
25 Remigius (d. 533)
26 Cedd (d. 664)
27 Frumentius (fourth century)
28 Simon the Zealot (first century)
28 Jude (first century, patron saint of the hopeless)
29 Narcissus (second century)
30 Marcellus (d. 298)
31 Wolfgang (ca. 930-994)

November

2 Victorinus (d. ca. 303)
3 Malachy (d. 1148)
3 Winefride (seventh century)
4 Vitalis (third century)
5 Bertille (d. 692)
6 Leonard (sixth century, patron saint of prisoners)
7 Willibrord (ca. 658-739)
9 Theodore the Recruit (d. 306)
10 Leo the Great (d. 461)
11 Martin of Tours (ca. 316-397, patron saint of beggars)
13 Abbo of Fleury (d. 1004)
13 Brice (d. 444)
13 Homobonus (d. 1197, patron saint of clothiers)
14 Lawrence (1128-1180)
15 Albert the Great (1206-1280)
16 Gertrude (d. 1302)
16 Margaret of Scotland (d. 1093)
17 Gregory of Tours (539-594)
17 Hilda (614-680)
17 Hugh (1140-1200)
18 Odo of Cluny (879-942)
19 Elizabeth of Hungary (1207-1231, patron saint of bakers)
20 Edmund (d. 870)
21 Columbanus (ca. 543-615)
22 Cecily (d. ca. 230, patron saint of church music)
23 Clement (d. 100)
25 Catherine (fourth century, patron saint of maidens)
27 James Intercisus (d. 421)
27 Virgil (d. 784)
29 Saturninus (d. ca. 257)
30 Andrew (first century)

December

1 Eligius (ca. 588-659, patron saint of blacksmiths)
2 Viviana (fourth century)
4 Barbara (fourth century, patron saint of architects)
4 Osmund (d. 1099)
5 Crispina of Tagora (d. 304)
5 Sabus (439-532)
6 Nicholas (d. ca. 342, patron saint of children)
7 Ambrose (ca. 340-397, patron saint of bishops and beekeepers)
8 Budo (sixth century)
9 Leocadia (d. 304)
10 Eulalia of Merida (d. ca. 304)
11 Damascus (306-384)
11 Daniel the Stylite (408-493)
12 Finnian (d. 549)
12 Walaric (d. 620)
13 Lucy (d. ca. 304, patron saint of eye disorders)
14 Spiridon of Corfu (fourth century)
16 Adelaide (931-999)
17 Olympias (ca. 368-410)
18 Samthann (d. 739)
19 Nemesion (d. 250)
20 Dominic of Silos (d. 1073)
22 Ischyrion (d. 250)
23 John of Kanti (1390-1473)
25 Anastasia (d. 304, patron saint of weavers)
26 Stephen (first century)
27 John (first century)
29 Thomas a Becket (1117-1170)
31 Sylvester (d. 335)

FOR FURTHER READING

D.C.O. Adams, *The Saints and Missionaries of the Anglo-Saxon Era.*

Peter Brown, *The Cult of the Saints: Its Rise and Function in Latin Christianity.*

Alban Butler, *Lives of the Saints.*

Patrick Geary, *Furta Sacra: Thefts of Relics in the Central Middle Ages.*

T.J. Heffernan, *Sacred Biography: Saints and Their Biographers in the Middle Ages.*

P. Paulus, *Indulgences as a Social Factor in the Middle Ages.*

Jonathan Sumption, *Pilgrimage: An Image of Medieval Religion.*

Victor and Edith Turner, *Image and Pilgrimage in Christian Culture.*

Jeanne Vielliard, trans., *Le guide de Pelerin de Saint-Jacques de Compostelle.*

Helen White, *Tudor Books of Saints and Martyrs.*

Stephen Wilson, *Saints and Their Cults: Studies in Religious Sociology, Folklore and History.*

CHAPTER TWENTY

CRUSADES

ope Urban II stood at the Council of Clermont in 1095 and began preaching for Christian knights not to kill each other, but to take the cross (a red cross was stitched onto their cloaks or surcoats) and drive the infidel from Christ's inheritance, meaning Jerusalem and the surrounding areas. The reasons for this are many — fear of the Muslims overrunning the Christian nations, a desire to unite the Byzantine East with the Roman West, a way to get the unruly younger sons of the nobility and knights out of Europe and to give them something worthwhile on which to expend their energies.

Though crusading remained popular, it wasn't without its critics. Some argued that Christians should hold with Christ and turn the other cheek. This idea was traditionally upheld by the Byzantines, but in the West, where war had played a more vital role, men often sought religious sanction for their warring natures. This tendency led the church to instigate the Leagues of Peace, Truce of God and other such writings to curb the warring people. Though most lay authorities aligned themselves to the idea of peace and abhorring war, many refused to adhere to it.

This reluctance is part of what led the church to redirect the energies of lay authorities away from each other and toward the Saracen threat. Men yielded to the church's call out of religious fervor (indulgences were granted for participants), desire for gold and land, because debts were postponed until a crusader returned, and for honor and glory, and other human reasons.

But they didn't just fight the Saracens. Over the next few centuries, crusades were fought for other reasons, such as to eradicate papal enemies and heretics. Jonathan Riley-Smith argues that the first crusade against papal enemies occurred in 1135 when Pope

Innocent II, " . . . granted an indulgence to those who fought the Normans and the anti-pope Anacletus."

The cost of crusading was high and many kings and powerful authorities went into debt for the sake of Holy War; an idea developed by St. Augustine in *City of God*:

> But the wise man, they say, will wage just wars. Surely, if he remembers that he is a human being, he will rather lament the fact that he is faced with the necessity of waging just wars; for if they were not just, he would not have to engage in them, and consequently there would be no wars for a wise man. For it is injustice of the opposing side that lays on the wise man the duty of waging wars; and this injustice is assuredly to be deplored by a human being, since it is the injustice of human beings, even though no necessity for war should arise from it.
>
> (trans. by Henry Bettenson in *City of God*, Penguin Books 1984).

Many men seized upon this notion of a divinely sanctioned war and used it for their own purposes.

The average cost of a knight going on crusade was four to five times his yearly income. Money was needed for care of his horses, pack animals, servants and armor. Money could be gained in a number of ways: taxation, sale of lands and goods, and loans. Dr. Elizabeth Hallam has stated that it would be virtually impossible for a landless knight to raise the money needed unless he was in the employ of a wealthier lord.

The height of crusading fervor was roughly 1187-1250. Though there were different types of crusades a knight could choose (against the infidel, papal enemies, heretics, etc.) the most preferred and prestigious was always that against the Saracens.

And while they sought to destroy the Holy Infidel, the crusaders ended up founding entire Christian cities in the East. Those who stayed called the Holy Land, Outremer (land beyond the sea). Such areas are: Edessa, Antioch, Tripoli and Jerusalem. However, these lands often shifted hands between the Christians and the Saracens.

❊ ❊ ❊

1096-1099 First Crusade: Peter the Hermit and Walter the Penniless led a group of poor, ill-armed men in an advance party, which was destroyed either on the trip or by Muslim soldiers when they reached Anatolia. The "real" army came out of France under the command of Baldwin of Flanders, Robert of Normandy, Godfrey de Bouillon and several others. They captured Antioch (June 3, 1098) and Jerusalem (July 15, 1099). They established four crusader states: Edessa, Tripoli, Jerusalem and Antioch.

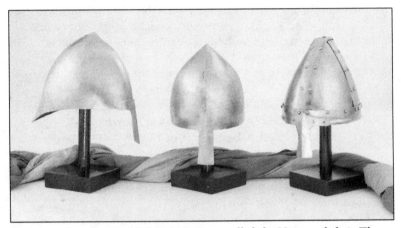

Various styles of conical helms (sometimes called the Norman helm). The conical helm was used throughout the Middle Ages, but would have been used mostly during the first two crusades.
(Used with permission from Museum Replicas Ltd.)

1146-1148 Second Crusade: Edessa fell to the Muslims in 1144. Prompted by Bernard of Clairvaux, Louis the VII (France) and Conrad III (Germany) led armies to the Holy Land. The Crusade was a disaster, but did manage to retake Lisbon, Portugal. Eleanor of Aquitaine also joined the venture and brought with her the Queen's Guard, which consisted of noblewomen dressed in armor.

1188-1192 Third Crusade: Saladin, the leader of the Muslim army, reconquered the Holy Land. Richard I (England), Philip II (France) and Frederick I (Germany) led troops. Frederick died on the way, but Leopold of Austria took command. Cyprus, Jerusalem, Acre, Ascalon and Jaffa were taken despite constant fighting and intrigue between the three commanders.

Typical garb of a soldier in the third, fourth and fifth crusades. The model wears a mail coif and hauberk, leather gauntlets (used mostly for riding), and holds a great helm, (now sometimes called the Crusader helm) popular from 1190 to around 1220.

(Used with permission from Museum Replicas Ltd.)

1202-1204 Fourth Crusade: Mostly French, they were diverted from the Holy Land and ended up taking Constantinople.

1209-1229 Albigensian Crusade: Fought in southern France against the Albigenses.

1212 Children's Crusade: Usually stated as a crusade of children and clerics led by Stephen of France and Nicholas of Germany. They supposedly met with death and slavery. However, historian Karen Armstrong in her book *Holy War* has proposed a new translation of the old texts. She claims the Crusade was nothing more than another religious upsurge in the countryside, which ended peacefully at the end of summer.

1217-1221 Fifth Crusade: Mostly French and led by Cardinal Pelagius, it was fought against Egypt. They took Damietta, but when they tried to take Egypt, they were cut off between Turkish troops and

Nile flood waters and were forced to surrender.

1228-1229 Sixth Crusade: Holy Roman Emperor Frederick II led a peaceful campaign in which he negotiated the return of Jerusalem, Lydda and Bethlehem.

1248-1254 Seventh Crusade: Led by Louis IX of France against Egypt. He retook Damietta without any fighting, but the overall effect of the expedition was the slaughter of thousands of his men.

1254-1292: Several small crusades were fought for a variety of reasons and by a gamut of people and countries.

1270 Eighth Crusade: Again led by Louis IX against Tunis, but he died before he could accomplish anything.

FOR FURTHER READING

Karen Armstrong, *Holy War: The Crusades and Their Impact on Today's World*.

Malcolm Billings, *The Cross and the Crescent: A History of the Crusades*.

Ernle Bradford, *The Great Betrayal: The Story of the Fourth Crusade*.

————— *The Sword and the Scimitar: The Saga of the Crusades*.

Alfred Duggan, *The Story of the Crusades 1097 to 1291*.

G.Z. Gray, *The Children's Crusade*.

Elizabeth Hallam, *Chronicles of the Crusades: Eye-witness Accounts of the Wars Between Christianity and Islam*.

Joinville and Villehardouin, *Chronicles of the Crusades*.

Harold Lamb, *The Crusades: Iron Men and Saints*.

Amin Maalouf, *The Crusades Through Arab Eyes*.

J.J. Robinson, *Dungeon Fire and Sword: The Knights Templar in the Crusades*.

Steven Runciman, *The First Crusade*.

Kenneth Setton, ed., *A History of the Crusades* (6 vols).

CHAPTER TWENTY-ONE

WEAPONS AND WAR

eapons and war were an integral part of the Middle Ages. But like everything else, warfare and weapons changed throughout the period. With every innovation in armor that protected the wearer, a new weapon would be created that could pierce it. Armorers always tried to stay one step ahead of the latest technology.

Though the church banned war upon unarmed peasants, clergy and the poor, not all men upheld the Peace of God that started ca. 975. This concept of peace was furthered by the Truce of God in around 1024 that banned war on specific days, including weekends and most holidays. Not content with the Peace and Truce of God, the church began preaching against Christians killing Christians, which led to the First Crusade and Pope Urban II sanctioning the Holy War against the Muslims.

Armies were small, usually no more than a few hundred. Most wars throughout this period consisted of small battles and raids. However, there were a few notable exceptions. It wasn't until the prominence of castles in the eleventh century that siege warfare began. This could be a tricky campaign, taking years and a fortune to complete.

✳ ✳ ✳

ARMOR TERMS

Acroc: A clasp.

Ailette: Used ca. 1250-1350, it tied on the shoulder and was used to display the coats of arms.

Aketon: Worn under mail (sometimes instead of), it was a padded or

---

TIME LINE OF ARMOR AND WEAPONRY

(dates are approximate)

500   Saxons use double-edged swords, helms, spears, round shields, axes, and short-sleeved byrnies that reach to the waist or mid-thigh.

800   Charlemagne's troops use lemallar armor.

800   Vikings also use lemallar armor.

1100   Crossbows are used.

1128   The helm is extended down the back to protect the neck.

1139   Pope Innocent II prohibits the use of crossbows against Christians.

1150   Surcoats appear.

1200   Great helm, kettle helm and helm with ear flaps appear.

1200   Plate pieces appear over mail.

1220   Skull cap appears and is worn beneath the helm or with a visor (not the same as the arming cap).

1250   Trebuchets are used.

1290   Longbow replaces the crossbow.

1300   Steel bows are introduced for the crossbow.

1330   Plate pieces cover most of the body.

1346   English use the first cannons against the French.

1400   Entire plate armor begins to appear.

1400   Primitive guns appear.

---

quilted garment. A number of materials could be used for the padding including grass or cloth.

Aiguilettes: The laces and tags that fastened armor together.

Anima: A type of splinted cuirass.

Arming Cap or Arming Bonett: A quilted cap that was worn beneath the coif or cervelliere.

Arming Doublet: Early fourteenth century. A quilted garment worn beneath the armor.

Arming Hose: Quilted hose worn beneath the chausses.

Arming Points: The ties that secured the armor into place.

Armor of Proof: Armor that could withstand an arrow.

Arret: Decorated tabs that appeared on armor straps.

Conical helm with nose guard, used throughout the Middle Ages.

(Used with permission from Museum Replicas Ltd.)

Great helm, popular from 1190 to around 1220. The great helm's flat top quickly grew unpopular since direct blows were absorbed by the helm rather than deflected.

(Used with permission from Museum Replicas Ltd.)

Sugarloaf great helm, popular from 1215 until the middle of the fourteenth century. The rounded top was more effective than the great helm at deflecting blows.

(Used with permission from Museum Replicas Ltd.)

(left) Pig-face basinet, popular from 1370 until the sixteenth century. (right) Burgonet with falling buffe, popular from the middle of the sixteenth century. (Used with permission from Museum Replicas Ltd.)

Arret de Lace: Lance rest.

Arsons (Arcons): The bow and cantle of the saddle.

Aventail: Mail attached around the base of a helm that covered and protected the shoulders.

Backplate: The plate that protected the back.

Bacul: Equestrian crupper.

Bard: Horse armor.

Basinet: A metal helm that enclosed the neck and face. Sometimes worn with a visor and aventail.

Batticuli: A plate that protected the loins.

Besagew: A round plate that covered that armpit.

Blanc haubert: Mail.

Bouche: The notch cut into the top of the shield where the lance rested.

Bow: The front part of the saddle.

Bracer: A piece of leather or cloth that protected an archer's arm from the string.

Breastplate: The front plate that covered the chest.

Breaths: The slits cut in the helm for ventilation.

Buckler: A small shield used by the infantry.

Bufie: A coat made from buffed leather.

Butts: An area used for archery practice.

Byrnie: Hauberk.

Camail: Mail attached around the base of a helm that covered and protected the shoulders.

Cannon: Armor worn over the arms.

Cantle: The rear of the saddle.

Chape: The metal piece at the bottom of a scabbard for a sword, dagger or knife that protected the bottom of the scabbard from wear.

Chapel de Fer: A wide-brimmed, open-faced helm.

Charnel: The bolt that secured the basinet to the breastplate.

Chausses, Chaussons: The mail pants or leggings.

Close Helmet: A helm that completely covered the head and face.

Coat Armor: A fourteenth-century garment worn over the armor for decorative purposes.

Codpiece: The mail or plate that covered the groin.

Coif: The mail worn over the head.

Couter: The plate for the elbow.

Crampon: A bolt that held the helm to the cuirass.

Crete, Cresta: The crest of the helm.

Crinet: The covering over the horse's neck.

Crupper: The covering for the horse's rump.

Crest: During the late thirteenth century, it was the heraldic device that topped the helm.

Cuirass: A paired back and breast plate. Could also denote body armor made of leather.

Cuir Bouilli: Armor made from leather that had been hardened by boiling with water or wax. Later used in tournaments instead of steel plates.

169

Cuisses: The covering for the thighs.

Damascening: A form of inlaying on metal.

Dossiere: The back of a cuirass.

Elbow Gauntlet: A gauntlet that reached all the way to the elbow.

Enarmes: The shield straps that enabled a knight to carry his shield.

Estival: Equestrian armor. Protected the horse's legs.

Exchange Pieces: Interchangeable pieces that enabled armor to be redesigned for battle and tourney without having to procure two different suits.

Fall: A shade over the brow of a helm.

Fan-Plate: The wing-like plate on the knee.

Fauld: Armor that protected the abdomen.

Fence: A tunic padded with plates.

Flanchard: Protected the horse's flanks.

Gadlings: The protruding studs on gauntlets.

Gambeson: Stuffed, quilted tunic either worn over, under or instead of armor.

Gamboised cuisses: Quilted, padded pieces that covered the thighs during the thirteenth century.

Garde-faude: Protected the groin.

Garde-rein: Covered the posterior.

Gauntlet: The armor or mail that covered the hand.

Glazing-wheel: The wheel used for polishing armor.

Gonfanon: Flag.

Gorget: The piece that covered the neck and shoulders.

A typical soldier's garb of the early 1300s. He wears a mail coif and halberk with articulated shoulder plates.

(Used with permission from Museum Replicas Ltd.)

Great Helm: The flat-topped, round helm introduced at the turn of the thirteenth century.

Greave: Covered the knee to the ankle.

Guard Chain: A chain that joined the helm, sword and dagger to the breastplate.

Guige: The strap that allowed a shield to be carried around the neck of the knight or squire.

Habergeon: A short hauberk.

Hauberk: A mail or scale tunic that reached to hip or knee depending on the period and fashion.

Haute Piece: The protruding neck guard attached to the shoulders.

Heaume: A heavy closed-visor helm used for tilting.

A close-up of articulated shoulder plates.

(Used with permission from Museum Replicas Ltd.)

Hosting Armor: War armor.

Hunskull: The English nickname for the pointed basinet visor that was popular during the late medieval period.

Jack: A leather tunic reinforced with metal plates or horn.

Jamb: Term used in the early period for greaves.

Jupon: Popular ca. 1340-1410, a padded garment used to display the wearer's coat of arms.

Kite-Shaped Shield: Popular from the tenth to thirteenth centuries, it was the long, almost triangular-shaped shield.

Lame: Pieces of steel that were used to join armor pieces.

Lamellar: Small metal plates that were laced together.

Lambrequin: A cloth hood that protected the neck from rain and heat.

List: An area used for war practice or designated for a tournament.

Mail: An interwoven suit of metal.

Mainfaire: The gauntlet for the right hand.

Main Gauche: A dagger used in the left hand while sword fighting with the right.

Manifer: Used mostly for a joust, it was a plate that covered and protected the lower left arm and hand.

Merlette: A staff carried by a sergeant.

Meris: A type of javelin.

Mezail: A visor.

Missodor: A war horse.

Mitten Gauntlet: A gauntlet where the fingers were not separated.

Muffler: The part of a mail hauberk that extended past the wrist and covered the hand. A slit was cut to enable the soldier to remove it and use his hands as needed.

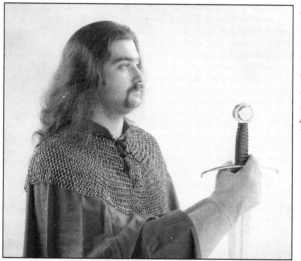

A chain mail bishop's mantle, used predominately by foot soldiers in the late Middle Ages.

(Used with permission from Museum Replicas Ltd.)

Munnions: Protected the shoulders and upper arms.

Nasal: The extension on a helm that protected the nose.

Niello: Black inlay used on plate.

Occularium: An eye-slit in a helm.

Orle: A garland worn beneath the crest on a helm.

Palet: Skull cap.

Panache: The plume on a helm.

Parement: Ceremonial dress.

Partlet: Gorget.

Pasguard: Reinforcement for the left elbow that was used while tilting.

Pauldron: Covered the shoulder and armpit.

Peytral: Equestrian armor that protected the chest.

Plates: A tunic lined with metal plates during the fourteenth century.

Pointille: A method of decorating armor that consisted of hammering a pattern of dots.

Poldermitton: Reinforced the right arm for a joust.

Poleyn: Protected the knee.

Pommel: Counterweight of the blade. Also the front rise of the bow.

Porte-panache: The attachment on the helm that held the panache in place.

Pot: Helm used by soldiers.

Rennen: Joust au pleasant where points were given for splintering lances, and victory was achieved by unhorsing the opponent.

Rennhut: Used for the rennen, it was a salade with a slit visor.

Renntartsche: A special shield used for the rennen. It fastened onto the breastplate to protect the knight.

Rennzeug: Term that refered to the rennen armor.

Rerebrace: Protected the upper arm.

Ringed Mail: Mail formed by sewing metal rings onto fabric or leather.

Rondel: The metal disc on staff weapons and daggers that guarded the hand from injury.

Sabaton (Solleret in French): Protected the foot.

Saddle Steel: A saddle with plate reinforcement on the cantle and bow.

Sallet or Salade: A lightweight helm that usually had a piece to cover the neck.

Scabbard: The sheath that protected swords and daggers.

Scale Armor: Plates or scales that were attached to cloth and that simulated scales.

Schynbalds: Worn over the mail, it protected the shin.

Shaffron (Chaffron): Equestrian armor that protected the horse's head.

Sight: The slit cut in a visor that enabled the knight to see.

Skull: A metal cap.

Spurs: Worn on the heel to prod the horse.

Stechhelm: A type of great helm worn during the getesch.

Stechsack: Used during the gestesch, it protected the knight's legs and the horse's chest.

Stechtartsche: Small shield used for the gestesch.

Stechzeug: Gestesch armor.

Stop Rib: A raised place in a plate to prevent a weapon from sliding into a weak joint and wounding the wearer.

Surcoat: Appeared in the twelfth century, it was a long- or short-sleeved, sometimes open-sided garment worn over armor.

Tabard: Worn by heralds, it displayed the coat of arms.

Tasset, Tace: Fifteenth-century piece that protected the thighs.

Tilt: Fifteenth-century development in the joust. It was the small fence that separated the jousters.

Tilting Socket: Used for the rennen, it hung from the saddle to protect the legs of the knight.

Toe-cap: The last piece of the sabaton.

Trapper: Equestrian protection made of leather. Knights would paint their coats of arms on it.

Vambrace: Protected the arm.

Ventail: Thirteenth-century innovation to the coif. It was a flap that wrapped around and protected the face.

Vevelles: Secured the aventail to the basinet.

Visor: Attached to the helm to protect the face.

Volant: Reinforcement for the brow.

WEAPONS

Alavica: A heavy spear.

Alborium: An eleventh-century bow made of hazelwood.

Alemele: Another name for a sword blade.

Ameure: A type of dagger.

Anelace: A type of fourteenth-century dagger that had a broad blade.

Arbalast a Cric: A heavy crossbow often used during sieges.

Arbalast a Cranequin: The type of crossbow that used a windlass to draw back the string.

Arbolest: A crossbow.

Arescuel: A lance's grip.

Arm: The part of a spur that enclosed the heel.

Armin: The ornamental grip of a pike.

Arming Sword: Sword used for thrusting and cutting.

Back Sword: A sword that had been sharpened on only one side — like a modern kitchen knife.

Ballista: A large siege machine used to fire huge spears at the enemy.

Barbed Arrowhead: An arrowhead with a barbed tip.

Bardiche: A type of pollaxe.

Baselard: A dagger.

Bastard sword: Long sword with a long hilt that could accommodate two hands.

Baston: A club with its head cut into a polygon shape.

Battering Ram: A fallen tree used to break open the doors of a castle.

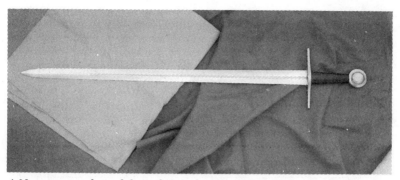

A Norman sword, used from the ninth century throughout the Middle Ages.
(Used with permission from Museum Replicas Ltd.)

Bec-de-faucon: An ax with a curve on one end that formed a point like the beak of a bird.

Belfrey: The wooden siege tower used to scale walls.

Bodkin: A slender arrowhead designed to pierce mail.

Bolt: Crossbow arrow.

Boson: An arrow with a blunted tip.

Boulon, Boujon: A type of arrow.

Brise-epee: Broken swords.

Broadhead: A type of wide arrowhead designed to maim when pulled out.

Caltrops: Spiked jack-like iron pieces designed to maim the foot of a horse or soldier.

Catapult: A large siege machine used to hurl objects over castle walls.

Champ-clos: An enclosed arena where two opponents met and fought during a tournament.

Coronel: The blunted piece that covered the tip of a lance during an au plaisant joust.

Coterel: A type of large knife.

Coursel: Windlass on a crossbow.

Crossbow: A mechanical bow.

A Scottish sword, ca. 1250.
(Used with permission from Museum Replicas Ltd.)

Crossguard: The part of the hilt that ran opposite the blade.

Dagger: Large, double-edged knife.

Dague a Orielles: Dagger that had a pommel shaped like the wings of a bird.

Dague a Ruelle: A dagger that had a thumb ring.

Destrier: Warhorse.

Dolon: A type of club.

Ecu: Shield.

Elingue: A sling.

Epieu: A spear that had a crossbar. Used for boar hunting where the bar protected the arms of the hunter.

Espringale: A large crossbow used for sieges that moved on wheels.

Estoc: A thrusting sword designed to stab.

Falarique: The arrowhead made of flammable material that was lit and shot.

Falchiona: A thirteenth century sword with a curved blade.

Falk: A scythe on a long spear.

Feather staff: A staff that had a spring release for a spike or set of spikes.

Foible: The tip of a blade.

Forte: The blade nearest the hilt.

Fuller: The center groove in a blade.

Fustibal: Used during sieges, it launched flaming projectiles.

Garrison: Where troops were lodged.

Garrock: A type of bolt.

Gibet: A mace.

Glaive: A bill with a large blade.

Guisarme: The long staff that had a crescent-shaped ax at the end.

Graffe: A type of small dagger.

Graper: The stop behind the lance's grip.

Greek Fire: A highly flammable compound that could burn even in water.

Grip: The handle of the sword or dagger.

Halague: A crossbowman.

Hampe: The staff of a bill.

Hars: Bow.

Heater Shield: The shape of shield most associated with the period. Dates ca. 1270.

Javelin: A throwing spear.

Lance: A charging spear that averaged fourteen feet. Made of wood, it usually had a steel tip.

Lance de Carriere: A lance used when tilting rings.

Lancegay: Light cavalry.

Locket: Sometimes used to fasten the scabbard to the sword belt, it was also the name of the metal circle that protected the top of the scabbard from the blade.

Longbow: Traditional English weapon that had a longer distance than a crossbow.

Loque: A staff.

Luchet: A pike.

Mace, Holy Water Sprinkler: A striking, club-like weapon with a metal-tipped end.

Mangonel: A machine used to throw stones.

Misericorde: Fourteenth-century term for a dagger.

Migerat: An arrow.

Nut: The round piece that held and cranked the string of a crossbow.

Pavise: The rectangular shield used to protect archers and infantry-men. Some may have had a prop to allow them to stand freely while the archer fired.

Passot: A dagger.

Patula: A short sword.

Pavade: A long dagger.

Pavon: A triangular flag.

Pell: A sharp stake used as a weapon by Norman peasants.

Pennon: Pointed banner used by knights.

Penthouse: The shed that was erected over a battering ram to protect soldiers.

Pike: A long spear.

Pile: Arrowhead.

Pitch: A black, tar-like compound that was heated and thrown on the enemy.

Polaxe: A long-handled axe.

Prick Spur: A simple spur with only one piece to prod the flanks.

Quarrel: Arrow.

Quarter Staff, Staff: A long pole used for fighting.

Quetyll: A knife.

Quicklime: White powder that could burn clothes and skin.

Quillons: The crossguard of a sword.

Raillon: A type of arrow.

Ranseur: A type of partizan.

Rowel: Star-shaped spur.

Semitarge: A scimitar.

Spight: A short arrow.

Stave: A long pole used as a weapon.

Stinkpot: A type of stink bomb made of sulphur and quicklime or a number of other ingredients. The mixture was placed in a small container and thrown into the face of an opponent.

Swordbreaker: A crenelated dagger that caught a sword blade and snapped it.

Tarcaire: A quiver.

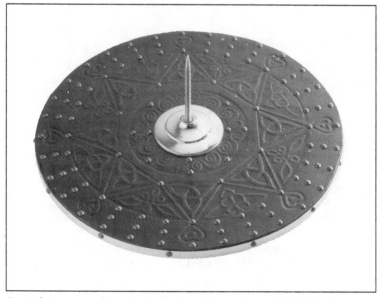

Scottish targe, used mostly in Scotland throughout the Middle Ages.
(Used with permission from Museum Replicas Ltd.)

The model holds a kite-shaped shield, used by the Normans from the early eleventh century, and later adapted by the English and used until the end of the Middle Ages. The model wears a Viking ceremonial horned helm with ear flaps.

(Used with permission from Museum Replicas Ltd.)

Target, Targe: Small shield.

Tarques: A siege weapon.

Tiller: The crossbow's stock.

Toggle: The crossbar on a spear.

Trebuchet: A type of catapult that used a counterweight to fire. It looked much like a giant slingshot.

Trigger: The release for the crossbow.

Trousse: A quiver.

Tuck: Nickname for estoc.

Umbo: Protected the hand that held the shield.

Undermine: The tunnel dug beneath a castle's wall to make it collapse.

Vamplate: The plate on a lance that protects the hand.

Vireton: A bolt that spins when it's shot from the crossbow.

Wifle: A practice sword.

IMPORTANT BATTLES AND WARS

841   Battle of Fontenoy. Fought between the sons of Charlemagne for control of Gaul. Resulted in the breakup of Charlemagne's empire.

843   Treaty of Verdun. Split Charlemagne's empire between his sons.

1066   Conquest of England. William the Conqueror invaded England with his Norman forces and set up Norman control.

1066   October 14: Battle of Hastings. Actually fought on the mound of Senlac. Norman troops defeated the English and killed King Harold, which opened the way for William to take the throne.

1195   October 7: Battle of Arsuf. Richard I and his crusaders defeated Saladin's reputed invincible army. Raised the morale of the troops and helped them successfully complete the Third Crusade.

1214   July 27: Battle of Bouvines. France defeated England and

Germany. It strengthened France's position and further eroded John's in England.

1259 December 4: Peace of Paris. Henry III surrendered Anjou, Maine, Normandy and Poitou, but retained Gascony. He was forced to pay homage to Louis IX of France.

1302 July 11: Battle of Courtrai. The Flemish beat France and allied to England. The ensuing conflicts and tension helped lead England and France into the Hundred Years' War.

1303 September 7: Humiliation of Anagni. Pope Boniface VIII was taken by Guillaume, highlighting the struggle between Rome and France.

1314 June 24: Battle of Bannockburn. The Scots defeated England, which broke the English yoke on their rule.

1320 Declaration of Arbroath. Robert the Bruce and other Scotsmen pledged themselves to independence.

1337- First segment of the Hundred Years' War marked by English victories.
1360

1346 August 26: Battle of Crecy. England defeated France.

1350s Jacquerie Rebellion. A peasant uprising in France marked by extreme bloodshed on both sides.

1360- Second segment of the Hundred Years' War marked by French victories.
1380

1378 Revolt of the Ciompi: The minor guilds rebelled against the major guilds and demanded equality. It worked for only a short time.

1380- Third segment of the Hundred Years' War marked by English triumphs.
1420

1381 The Great Revolt. English peasant uprising. Wat Tyler leads the protest against unfair taxation. Marching toward London, the peasants were headed off by Richard II.

1415 October 25: Battle of Agincourt. Fought between England and France, it was a major battle of the Hundred Years' War where the English soundly defeated the French.

1420- The fourth and last segment of the Hundred Years' War, which solidified both English and French nationalism.
1453

1455- Wars of the Roses. Civil war between the Lancasters and the Yorks. Ended with the success of Henry Tudor (VII).
1489

FOR FURTHER READING

Philippe Contamine, *War in the Middle Ages*.

Hans Delbruck, *Medieval Warfare*.

Christopher Gravett, *Medieval Siege Warfare*.

T.E. Griess, *Ancient and Medieval Warfare*.

David Harding, ed., *Weapons: An International Encyclopedia from 5000 B.C. to 2000 A.D.*

Ian Heath, *Armies of the Middle Ages* (2 vols).

Tim Newark, *The Barbarians: Warriors and Wars of the Dark Ages*.

————— *Medieval Warfare*.

A.V.B. Norman and D. Pottinger, *English Weapons and Warfare 449 to 1660*.

Desmond Seward, *The Hundred Years' War*.

R.C. Smail, *Crusading Warfare, 1097 to 1193*.

Philip Warner, *Sieges of the Middle Ages*.

Terrence Wise, *Saxon, Viking and Norman*.

prent. l'x sea espules. a[...]
t. tota dur. biaus fanur.
a aesta et aparellie se li d[...]
moi sire chr. et il li fist er,
rour au siege pullens. de le
s. et beue le dias dont il en[...]
[...] u uur fere [...] le [...]
[...]sseur a est [...] gu[...]
no regarc [...] leuree [...]
[...]es lenom as[...] [...]
[...]ent. Sur. chr. asrer ue[...]
[...]ur [...] sufis rot [...]
[...] apcome [...]
[...]er ana fer ee [...] ua[...]
luna mor [...] a ua[...]
[...] a[...]

PART FOUR

People & Places

CHAPTER TWENTY-TWO

THE SAXONS

The Angles and Saxons began their invasion into England during the final days of the Roman Empire and within 150 years, they dominated their new land. Though their language was Germanic in origin, it was always referred to as English whether spoken by the Saxons, Jutes or Angles.

Christianity came first to England during its Roman days, but due to the customs of its new Saxon kings, Christianity fell out of fashion. Missionaries reappeared during the sixth century, and over the next hundred years, they slowly began to reconvert the English.

We find the term *Engla Lande* (Land of the Angles) used around 880. By this time, the Viking invaders had already been to England's shores several times. Their constant raids led them to settle York, East Anglia and Mercia. Once settled, they forced the English to buy them off with treasure called Danegeld. Should any English person encounter a Viking, the English person had to cede the road or bridge and call the Viking "Lord" or "Lady Dane." Not satisfied with these accomplishments, the Vikings continued to attack the English natives, until King Alfred led his rebellion and began reclaiming lost territory. For a while, Alfred confined them to a large area known as the Danelaw.

Though the Danes did continue to fight for dominance over England, the English themselves became more independent and began developing their own culture, law and language until the Norman invasion of 1066, when their customs were absorbed and altered by their new conquerors.

❈ ❈ ❈

188

VOCABULARY

Aefen: Evening.

Aernemergen: Early morning.

Alderman: Noble.

Andsaca: Enemy.

Anforht: Terrified.

Anhaga: Solitary.

Anwealda: Lord.

Atheling: Prince.

Attor: Venom.

Bana: Slayer.

Beadurinc: Warrior.

Bearn: Child.

Beorn: Man.

Bileofa: Food.

Bill: Sword.

Bilwit: Innocent.

Boga: Bow.

Bordweall: Shield-wall.

Breostcofa: Heart.

Bretwalda: Ruler of the Britons.

Brimmann: Viking.

Burh: Fort.

Burnsele: Bathing area.

Byrne: Coat of mail.

Byrnwiga: Armored warrior.

Cald: Cold.

= Celtic Areas

Strathclyde
(Cumbria)

Northumbria

Mercia

Cambria
(North Wales)

East
Anglia

Damnonia
(West Wales)

West Saxonia
(Wessex)

East Saxonia
(Essex)

Londinium

South Saxonia
(Sussex)

Cantia
(Kent)

Map of early 7th century Britain.
Areas of Celtic concentration are highlighted.

Carcern: Prison.

Ceorl, Churl: Peasant.

Cicen: Chicken.

Cild: Child.

Cirice: Church.

Cnapa: Servant.

Cniht: Servant, boy, youth.

Cwen: Queen.

Cwene: Woman.

Cynelic: Noble.

Cynerice: Kingdom.

Cyning: King.

Cynn: Family.

Cyssan: Kiss.

Cyst: Best.

Daeg: Day.

Dene: Danes.

Denisc: Danish.

Deofol: Devil.

Deore: Beloved.

Derian: Harm.

Dogor: Day.

Dohtor: Daughter.

Dol: Foolish.

Dolg: Wound.

Draca: Dragon.

Dreng: Viking warrior.

Dreorig: Sad.

Dyrne: Secret.

Eafora: Son.

Eald: Old.

Ealdorman: Nobleman.

Eam: Uncle.

Earh: Cowardly.

Eorcanstan: Jewel.

Eorl: Nobleman.

Eoten: Giant.

Faeder: Father.

Faeger: Beautiful.

Faemne: Maiden.

Fea: Little.

Feond: Enemy.

Flan: Arrow.

Forht: Fear.

Fracod: Vile.

Freond: Friend.

Fyrd: Army.

Fyrdman: Soldier.

Gast: Angel (m).

Gebiddan: Pray.

Geboren: Brother.

Gewinnan: Conquer.

Gyst: Stranger.

Hafoc: Hawk.

Hatheort: Impulsive.

Heofen: Heaven.

Heriot: Cash or war gear paid for the death of a soldier.

Hlaford: Lord, master.

Holm: Sea.

Holt: Forest.

Hordcofa: Heart.

Hwitel: Knife.

Ides: Woman.

Leasung: Lying.

Leod: Prince.

Leof: Dear.

Lind: Shield.

Lytling: Child.

Maeg: Kinsman.

Mage: Kinswoman.

Mandrinc: Poison.

Mearh: Horse.

Middaeg: Midday.

Middeneaht: Midnight.

Modcearu: Heart grief.

Mondryhten: Liege lord.

Nieten: Beast.

Nithing: Coward.

Preost: Priest.

Sar: Pain, wound.

Scand: Shame.

Scima: Light.

Seax: Dagger or sword.

Sefa: Heart.

Serf: Unfree peasant.

Sinc: Treasure.

Skeggox: A hand ax used as a throwing weapon or in hand-to-hand combat.

Snaw: Snow.

Snell: Bold.

Steorra: Star.

Sweltan: Die.

Sweoster: Sister.

Swetmete: Sweetmeat.

Swetnis: Sweetness.

Swigian: Hush.

Thane: Landowner.

Treow: Faith, truth.

Undeadlic: Immortal.

Unryht: Unjust.

Waed: Water.

Waedbrec: Breeches.

Waelraest: Death in battle.

Weard: Guardian.

Wer: Husband.

Wergeld: Price paid according to rank for the wrongful death of a person.

Wergeldthief: A criminal whose crimes were paid for by a wergeld.

Wiccecraeft: Witchcraft.

Wifian: Marry.

Wilddeor: Wild beast.

Willan: Will, desire.

Wine: Friend.

Winedryhten: Beloved lord.

Wuldorfaeder: God.

Wulf: Wolf.

Wyf: Wife.

Wynlic: Joyful.

Wynn: Joy.

Wyrm: Worm.

Yfel: Evil.

Ylfetu: Swan.

FOR FURTHER READING

P.H. Blair, *Roman Britain and Early England 55 B.C. to A.D. 871.*
——————— *An Introduction to Anglo-Saxon England.*
Christopher Brooke, *From Alfred to Henry III 871 to 1272.*
David Brown, *Anglo-Saxon England.*
John Clark, *Saxon and Norman London.*
Kevin Crossley-Holland, *The Anglo-Saxon World: An Anthology.*
D.J.V. Fisher, *The Anglo-Saxon Age ca. 400 to 1042.*
G.N. Garmonsway, *The Anglo-Saxon Chronicle.*
Geoffrey of Monmouth, *The History of the Kings of Britain.*
Christopher Gravett, *Hastings 1066: The Fall of Saxon England.*
Dick Hamilton, *Lawyers and Lawbreakers.*
John Haywood, *Dark Age Naval Power.*
David Hill, *An Atlas of Anglo-Saxon England.*
David Howarth, *1066 the Year of the Conquest.*
Lloyd and Jennifer Laing, *The Origins of Britain.*
K.J. Leyser, *Rule and Conflict in an Early Medieval Society.*
B. Lyon, *A Constitutional and Legal History of Medieval England.*
H.A. MacDougall, *Racial Myth in English History: Trojans, Teutons, and Anglo-Saxons.*

C.T. Onions, ed., *Sweet's Anglo-Saxon Reader*.
Beram Saklatvala, *The Origins of the English People*.
L.M. Smith, ed., *The Making of Britain: The Dark Ages*.
———— *The Making of Britain: The Middle Ages*.
F.M. Stenton, *Anglo-Saxon England*.
Edwin Tetlow, *Hastings* (also known as *The Enigma of Hastings*).
John Wacher, *The Coming of Rome*.
Dorothy Whitelock, *The Beginnings of English Society*.
Ralph Whitlock, *The Warrior Kings of Saxon England*.

Folklore
Geoffrey Ashe, *The Discovery of King Arthur*.
Henry Bett, *English Myths and Legends*.
Chretien de Troyes, *Arthurian Romances*.
N.L. Goodrich, *Guinevere*.
———— *King Arthur*.
———— *Medieval Myths*.
———— *Merlin*.
Christine Hole, *English Folk Heroes*.
J.C. Holt, *Robin Hood*.
Andrea Hopkins, *Chronicles of King Arthur*.
R.S. Loomis, *The Grail*.
P.M. Matarasso, *The Quest of the Holy Grail*.

CHAPTER TWENTY-THREE

VIKINGS

The origin of the word *Viking* is rather obscure. The Oxford English Dictionary suggests it probably came from the Anglo-Saxon term *wic* which means "camp." Other sources claim the word is from Old Norse meaning "to raid" or from the Norse *vik* meaning "creek." At any rate, the term was used during the eighth century in England, though the Danes themselves didn't use the term until later.

The great age of the Vikings is ca. 800 to 1100. For reasons unknown, during this time, the Scandinavian people began journeying from their homes and preying on Europe. During their first wave of attacks, they settled in Ireland, France, England and the Shetland and Orkney Islands. These attacks reached as far as Iceland and the Mediterranean.

Great sailors and fighters, the Vikings had main ports, such as Hedeby and Birka, where they traded slaves and other items. When it came to working with textiles and metal, Viking crafters were some of the best to be found.

As a main home base, the Swedish Vikings controlled Finland, Norwegian Vikings controlled the Orkney and Shetland Islands, and the Danish Vikings controlled the Dutch coast. During their ninth-century excursions, the Norwegians went into England (where some of the Danes contributed), Greenland, Frankia and Ireland.

During the tenth century, some of the Vikings were beginning to bring Christianity back to their people. But it was Olav Trygvasson who helped convert the homeland, and for the Vikings who settled in Normandy, conversion was mandatory.

⚜ ⚜ ⚜

NORSE MYTHOLOGY

Alberich: A dwarf.

Alf: Dead and living in the underworld.

Alfrigg: A dwarf.

Andvaranaut: Brunhild's ring.

Andvari: Treasure guardian.

Angerbotha, Angerboda, Angrboda: A giant.

Arvakl: A horse.

Asgard: City of the gods.

Atli: King of the Huns.

Aud: Son of night.

Audhumbla, Audumla: A giant cow that nursed Ymir.

Balder, Baldur, Baldr: Son of Odin.

Balmung: Siegfried's sword.

Bergelmir: A giant.

Bestla: Mother of Odin.

Bifrost: The bridge from earth to Asgard.

Bolthor: A giant.

Bolverk: A disguise of Odin.

Bor: Father of Odin.

Borghild, Borghlide, Borghilda: Wife of Sigmund.

Bori: Father of Bor.

Bragi: God of poetry.

Branstock: A tree in Volsung's palace.

Brisingamen: Freya's necklace.

Brokk: A dwarf.

Dain: A dwarf.

Draupnir: Odin's magic ring.

Draupnir: Armlet of Odin.

Durin: A dwarf.

Eggther: Guardian for the giants.

Eitri: A dwarf.

Elli: A giant.

Erna: Wife of Jarl.

Fafnir, Fafner: A dragon.

Fasolt: Killed by Fafnir.

Fenrir, Fenris-wolf, Fenris: A monster wolf.

Fjorgyn: Mother of Thor.

Forseti: Son of Balder.

Freki: Odin's wolf.

Frey, Freyr: God of weather.

Freya: Goddess of love.

Frigga: Goddess of matrimonial love.

Fulla: One of Frigga's ladies in waiting.

Garm: Guarded the gate of Hel.

Geirrod: Brother of Geirrid.

Gimle: New heaven.

Ginnungagap: The abyss that birthed all living things.

Gjallar: Horn sounded for Ragnorok.

Gjalp: A giant.

Gleipnir: Magic net woven to hold Fenrir.

Glistenheath: The place where Sigurd killed Fafnir.

Gna: One of Frigga's ladies-in-waiting.

Gram: Sigurd's sword.

Greip: A giant.

Greyfell: Sigurd's horse.

Grid: Wife of Odin.

Grimhild, Grimhilda, Grimhilde: Mother of Gudrun.

Gullinbursti: The boar ridden by Freyr.

Gulltopp: The horse of Heimdall.

Gullveig: A witch.

Gungir: Odin's spear.

Gunnlod: Mother of Bragi.

Gunther: Brother of Kriemhild.

Guttorm: Brother of Gudrun.

Gymir: Father of Gerd.

Hagen: Killed Siegfried.

Heidrun: The goat who supplied mead for the gods.

Heimdal: Guardian of Bifrost.

Hel, Hela: Goddess of the underworld.

Hermod: Messenger of the gods.

Hilde, Hild, Hilda, Hildur: A Valkyrie.

Hiordis: Second wife of Sigmund.

Hoder, Hodur, Hodr: Blind son of Odin.

Hoenir, Honir: Brother of Odin.

Hreidmar: Dwarf king.

Hrimfaxi: Horse of night whose bridle dripped the morning dew.

Hugi: A giant.

Hvergelmir: The home of Nidhug.

Hyndla: A giant.

Hyrrokkin: An ogre.

Jarnsaxa: A giant.

Jord: Daughter of Night.

Jormungand: The serpent who encircled the earth.

Kriemhild, Kriemhilda, Kriemhilde: Wife of Siegfried.

Lidskjalf: Throne of Odin.

Lin: One of Frigga's ladies-in-waiting.

Lodur: Giver of senses.

Lofn: Goddess of lust.

Lofnheid, Lyngheid: Sister of Otter.

Loki: God of destruction and mischief.

Magni: One of the seven gods of the Aesir.

Menglad: Won by Svipdag.

Mista: A Valkyrie.

Mjolnir, Miolnir: Thor's hammer.

Modi: Son of Thor.

Munin: Memory.

Nagelfar: The ship that carried the dead to Ragnarok.

Nanna: Wife of Balder.

Nerthus: Mother of earth.

Nidhug, Nidhogg: A dragon.

Njord: Father of Freya.

Noss: Daughter of Frey.

Odin, Othin, Od: God of the sky, king of the gods.

Ragnarok: The final battle of the gods.

Ran: A sea goddess.

Regin: A blacksmith.

Rinda, Rind: A giant.

Rungnir: A giant killed by Thor.

Saehrimnir: A magic boar.

Saga: Drank with Odin in her hall.

Sangrida: A Valkyrie.

Sif: Thor's second wife.

Sign, Sigun, Signy: Daughter of Volsung.

Sigyn: Wife of Loki.

Sinfiotli: Son of Siggeir.

Sinmora: Wife of Surt.

Skade: Goddess of skiers.

Skidbladnir: The magical ship of Freyr.

Skinfaxi: Stallion of the daylight.

Skirnir: A servant of Freyr.

Skrymir: King of the giants.

Skuld: Norn of the future.

Sleipnir: Odin's horse.

Snotra: Self-discipline.

Starkadhr: A fierce warrior.

Svaldifari: A stallion.

Swanhild, Swanhilda, Swanhilde: Daughter of Sigurd.

Syn: Invoked during trials.

Tarnkappe: A cloak that rendered its wearer invisible.

Thaukt: A giant.

Thialfi, Thjalfi: A servant of Thor.

Thir: Wife of Thrall.

Thokk: A female disguise Thor used to protect himself from Balder.

Thor: God of thunder.

Thrym: A giant.

Tjasse: A giant.

Tyr, Tiu: God of war.

Ull: God of skiers.

Urd: Norn of the past.

Utgard-Loki: A king of the giants.

Vali: Son of Odin.

Valkyrie: Freya's priestesses.

Vanir: A god of rain.

Var: Punished adulterers.

Ve: Giver of feeling.

Verdandi: Norn of the present.

Vili: Giver of reason.

Volva: A prophetess.

Vor: An omniscient goddess.

Yggsdrasil: The tree that bound Heaven, Hel and earth.

Ymir: A giant.

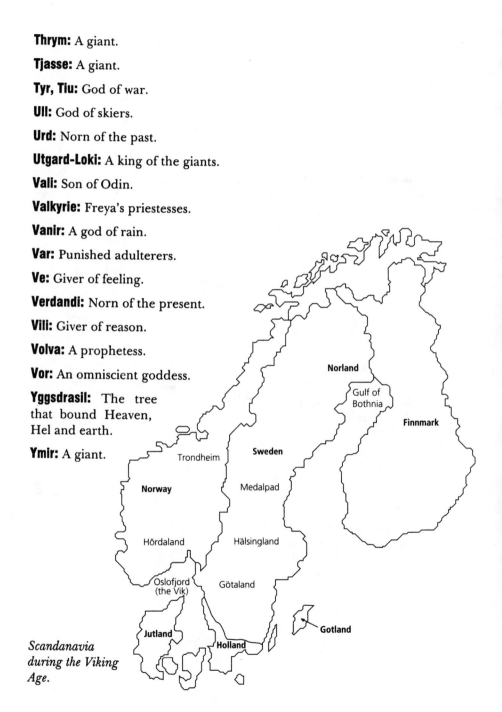

Scandanavia during the Viking Age.

FOR FURTHER READING

Viking Religion
David Bellingham, *An Introduction to Norse Mythology*.
Brian Branston, *Gods of the North*.
D.J. Conway, *Norse Magic*.
Kevin Crossle-Holland, *The Norse Myths*.
H.R. Ellis Davidson, *Gods and Myths of Northern Europe*.
Ed Fitch, *The Rites of Odin*.
Jacob Grimm, *Teutonic Mythology*.
H.A. Guerber, *Myths of Northern Lands: Narrated with Special Reference to Literature and Art*.
Viktor Rydberg, *Teutonic Mythology: Gods and Goddesses of the Northland*.
Tre Tryckare, *The Viking*.
Gabriel Turville-Petre, *Myth and Religion of the North: The Religion of Ancient Scandinavia*.

General History
A.W. Brogger and H. Shetelig, *The Viking Ships*.
Johannes Bronsted, *The Vikings*.
Yves Cohat, *The Vikings: Lords of the Seas*.
P.G. Foote and D.M. Wilson, *The Viking Achievement*.
Gwyn Jones, *A History of the Vikings*.
T.D. Kendrick, *A History of the Vikings*.
F.D. Logan, *The Vikings in History*.
H.R. Loyn, *The Vikings in Britain*.
Magnus Magnusson and Hermann Palsson, *Njal's Saga*.
———— *Laxdaela Saga*.
———— *The Vinland Sagas*.
P.H. Sawyer, *The Age of the Vikings*.
Jacqueline Simpson, *Everyday Life in the Viking Age*.
Snorri Sturluson, *King Harald's Saga*.
———— *The Prose Edda*.
———— *The Poetic Edda*.
———— *Heimskringla*.
Edred Thorsson, *Northern Magic*.
Tre Tryckare, *The Viking*.
D.M. Wilson, *Civil and Military Engineering in Viking Age Scandinavia*.
———— *The Vikings and Their Origins*.

CHAPTER TWENTY-FOUR

FRANCE AND NORMANDY

n 58 B.C. the Romans under the command of Julius Caesar invaded Gaul. Due to the dissension between the Celtics and other tribes who lived there, Gaul quickly fell and was ruled by Rome for the next five hundred years.

Under Rome's banner, the people shifted from hut builders into civilized society where art, literature, trade and politics became important. Missionaries moved in and began converting the citizens from their pagan roots to Christianity (this was a long process).

For a time, it appeared as if Gaul might become unified. But with the collapse of Rome so went all unity. The split was furthered by invasions from a number of hostile groups such as the Vandals, Teutons, Franks, Goths and Burgundians. In the end, it was Clovis (converted to Christianity in 496) who in 481 rose victorious and founded the Merovingian rulership of the Frankish Kingdom which lasted until 751. Clovis is also the first to claim Paris as his capital.

For just over three hundred years, the descendants of Clovis reigned in the Frankish Kingdom, but by the eighth century it was clear that the Merovingians were more incompetent than kingly. In 751 Pepin the Short, a Carolingian, succeeded in gaining Pope Zacharias' support, and he effectively removed Childeric III, the Merovingian king, from the Frankish throne. For the next 240 years, the Carolingians ruled the Frankish state.

The Frankish empire reached its height under Charlemagne who instituted education and early feudalism. But after his death, his successors followed in the footsteps of the Merovingians, and in 987 Hugh Capet was crowned beginning the Capetian line of kings. However, the title of King of the Franks was a matter of debate.

Never a homogenous region, each duchy of France fell more under the control of its duc or count than under any real royal influence. After the death of Charlemagne and until the Hundred Years War, the French king had little to no authority outside of the Ile de France. The only notable exception to this was Philip Augustus who, in the thirteenth century, was able to exercise a great deal of control. But despite the ground he won, succeeding kings were never able to achieve the same degree of control as existed in other countries.

It is rather ironic that the concept of feudalism grew up in a region infamous for its weak monarchy. Instead of the pinnacle of the feudalistic pyramid being the king, it was the local prince or duc. For this reason, I encourage researchers to examine the region where their book takes place.

NORMANDY

Viking raids in the tenth century led Charles III of the Frankish kingdom to buy peace by sectioning off Northwest France around Rouen and giving it to the Viking chieftain Rollo in 911. In less than one hundred years, the so-called Viking settlers had adapted to their new culture so well that very few even spoke their native tongue. They seized upon the Frankish customs and made them their own.

The unstable conditions in France combined with the country's native warrior roots produced a new breed of fighter — the Norman soldier. Trained with the latest technology of horse-warfare and castle building, the soldiers were more than a match for the English in 1066 when William the Conqueror led his famous campaign. An added incentive was their relatively open social mobility. To gain land and status, all a low-born fighter had to do was accompany and aid his lord in battle knowing his lord would reward his faithful service.

And within fifty years (1050-1100), different bands of Normans brought England, Sicily and southern Italy under their control, not to mention their heavy involvement with the first two crusades.

❊ ❊ ❊

VOCABULARY

Ange: Angel.

Antrustiones: Bodyguards of the Merovingians.

Dame: Lady.

Damoiselle: Damsel.

Destrier: Warhorse.

Diable: Devil.

Enfeoff: Invest.

Esprit Malin: Evil one.

Frere: Brother.

Heriot: The inheritance tax gathered by the Carolingians.

Ma: My. Used for feminine words.

Malfaisance: Wicked.

Mechant: Evil.

Mere, Maman: Mother.

Miles: Knight.

Missi: Representative sent from the royal court.

Mon: My. Used for masculine words.

Pere: Father.

Seigneur: Lord.

Soeur: Sister.

FOR FURTHER READING

D. Bates, *Normandy before 1066*.
Tania Bayard, trans., *A Medieval Home Companion*.
R.A. Brown, *The Normans*.
G. Duby, *Medieval Marriage: Two Models from Twelfth-Century France*.
———— *The Knight, the Lady and the Priest*.
———— *The Age of Cathedrals: Art and Society 980 to 1420*.
Ian Dunlop, *Burgundy*.
Einhard and Notker the Stammerer, *Two Loves of Charlemagne*.
Robert Fawtier, *The Capetian Kings of France: Monarchy and Nation 987 to 1328*.
France and Joseph Gies, *Life in a Medieval City*.
Jean Gimpel, *The Cathedral Builders*.

Gregory of Tours, *The History of the Franks*.

E.M. Hallam, *Capetian France 987 to 1328*.

Charles H. Haskins, *The Normans in European History*.

E.L. Ladurie, *Montaillou: The Promised Land of Error*.

Nicholas Michael, *Armies of Medieval Burgundy 1364 to 1477*.

J.J. Norwich, *The Normans in the South*.

Sidney Painter, *French Chivalry*.

J. le Patourel, *The Norman Empire*.

Katharine Scherman, *The Birth of France: Warriors, Bishops and Long-Haired Kings*.

CHAPTER TWENTY-FIVE

SCOTLAND

C aledonia, or Scotland as we know it today, resisted the Roman invasion around A.D. 120 which resulted in the construction of Hadrian's Wall that separated Roman-held England from the turbulent North. At that time, two groups were predominant in Scotland—the Picts and the Celts.

Over the next two hundred years, Britons began migrating into the southern parts of Scotland. By the fourth century, they held Northumbria, Strathclyde and Dumbarton. Early Scotland was divided among the Picts in the far north, the Irish and Scots on the West Coast, and the Angles in the south. Britons had settled in the areas already mentioned.

For a time, the English and Irish raided surrounding lands, conquering much of Pictland, but in 685 the English were defeated and pushed out. Over the next few centuries, the Irish, Scots and Pictish royal families intermarried (inheritance was traced through the mother, not the father), and the Vikings raided and settled into the area where they remained until their expulsion in the thirteenth century.

Though there were a few kings who claimed to be king of Pictland and the Irish lands, it wasn't until Kenneth MacAlpin in 843 that Scotland had a true king. From this time on, Scotland was unified.

Throughout the tenth and eleventh centuries, Scotland and England raided and battled for control of the border regions. However, Scotland's strong eleventh-century kings were able to maintain their freedom even against the Normans who now claimed the Scots owed them fealty.

But by 1290, Scotland had fallen into disarray. The death of Queen Margaret ended the line of Malcolm Canmore and with no direct heir and a number of claimants, Scotland found itself in the middle of a nasty affair.

Edward I of England saw his opportunity. He offered to settle the debate—for a price of course—and he named John Balliol the new king. The Scottish accepted John but were not about to bow before the English heel on other matters. John refused to give into the English monarch. In 1296, Edward took control of Scotland, but a number of commanders rebelled. One of the most famous rebels was Robert the Bruce, who at the Battle of Bannockburn settled the matter by defeating Edward's army.

After Robert's death in 1329, England renewed its claims of sovereignty. But the outbreak of the Hundred Years' War with France in 1337 complicated the issue, drawing attention away from Scotland.

Then in 1371 the first Stewart, Robert II, took the Scottish throne. Strife and conflict with England continued until the two thrones were united by John I of England (John VI of Scotland) in 1603.

❖ ❖ ❖

VOCABULARY

Ablach: Dwarf or one who was unimportant.

Aboon: Over or above.

Acquent: Acquaint.

Aiblins: Maybe.

Airn: Iron.

Ane: One.

Aneuch: Enough.

Athair: Father.

Atweel: Certain.

Atweel na: Certainly not.

Aught: Anything.

Auld: Old.

Aumous: Alms.

Awee: Little.

Bairn: Child.

Bairned: Pregnant.

Ban: To swear.

Bannock: Flat bread.

Barkit: Dirty.

Barmkin: A wall that enclosed.

Baudrons: Cat.

Bawbee: Halfpenny.

Bawds: Rabbit.

Ben: Inside.

Beuk: Book.

Birse: Impudent.

Bizzem: A promiscuous woman.

Blae: Angry.

Blate: Shy.

Blaw: Boast.

Blether: Idle chatter.

Bock: Regurgitate.

Bodach: Old man.

Bogle: Ghost.

Bonnie: Stout.

Brathair: Brother.

Braw: Handsome.

Bretasche: A walkway on a castle wall.

Brogue: Shoe.

Brose: Porridge.

Buirdly: Broad shouldered.

Busk: To dress.

But-an-ben: Small cottage.

Cailin: Damsel.

Caird: Sturdy beggar.

Canna: Can't.

Cannie: Gentle.

Cantie: Happy.

Cantrip: A spell.

Carlin: An old woman.

Cauld: Cold.

Caur: A calf.

Chapman: Peddler.

Chiel: Youth.

Clachan: Small village.

Claid heamh: Sword

Claid mor: Broadsword.

Claid crom: Sabre.

Claid caol: Small sword.

Claik: Gossip.

Claymore: Traditional two-handed sword.

Clishmaclaver: Idle chatter.

Close: A courtyard that linked several buildings.

Clootie: Devil.

Coggie: Wooden dish.

Connached: Destroyed, abused.

Cooser: Stallion.

Couthie: Loving.

Croft: Craft.

Cuif: Foolish.

Daffin: Happy.

Daith: Death.

Dander: Wander.

Dinna: Don't.

Doitit: Stupid.

Doocot: Dovecote.

Dother, Dochter: Daughter.

Doup: Buttocks.

Dour: Stubborn.

Dowie: Sad.

Farl: Oatcake.

Fash: Trouble.

Fasheous: Troublesome.

Feckless: Tiny.

Feu: Land grant.

Feuar: Vassal.

Feu-duty: Annual payment made to a feudal overlord.

Fore: A forebuilding that protected the entrance way.

Glaikit: Thoughtless.

Glaives: Swords.

Gleg: Sharp.

Gloamin: Evening.

Greetin: Crying.

Guidman: Husband.

Hale: Healthy.

Hansel: Special gift.

Haugh: Meadow.

Hosen: Hose.

Hurdies: Hips.

Ingle: Fire.

Jimp: Slender.

Kelpie: Demon.

Ken: To know.

Kenspeckle: To stand out.

Kirk: Church.

Kittle: Difficult.

Kye: Cow.

Laich: Low.

Laird: Landholder.

Lickit: Beaten.

Loan: Path.

Loch: Lake.

Loon: Boy.

Lowe: Flame.

Luckie: Middle-aged woman.

Lug: Ear.

Lyart: Gray.

Mairrit: Married.

Mathair: Mother.

Maukin: Rabbit.

Mattucashlass: A dagger worn under the armpit.

Maun: Must.

Maunna: Mustn't.

Mirk: Dark.

Ni: No.

Nicht: Night.

Nickum: Mischievous.

Nocht: Nothing.

Outspeckle: To stand out.

Paughty: Haughty.

Paukie: Cunning.

Piuthar: Sister.

Pleasaunce: A walled garden.

Plisky: Trick.

Pree: To kiss.

Pree'd: Kissed.

Puddock: Frog.

Quean: Young woman.

Ratton: A rat.

Reivers: Cattle raiders.

Riven: Torn.

Sark: Shirt.

Scaith: Hurt.

Scunner: To sicken.

Shalt: Pony.

Shieling: Small cottage.

Skirl: Scream.

Skirtit: Run quickly.

Sloken: To quench.

Soo: Sow.

Spae: Foretell.

Spaewife: Fortune-teller.

Steading: Grouped farm buildings.

Stot: Ox.

Streen: Yesterday.

Sumph: Stupid, soft.

Swank: Lithe, tall.

Swither: To hesitate.

Taet: Little.

Taupie: A stupid young woman.

Thole: To suffer.

Tint: Lost.

Tocher: Dowry.

Tod: Fox.

Tow: Rope.

Trews: Pants.

Unco: Rude, peculiar.

Wad: Would.

Wadna: Wouldn't.

Wae: Woe.

Wat, Weet: Wet.

Weans: Children.

Weeda: Widow.

Ween: Think.

Werna: Weren't.

Whinger: Dirk.

Whingin': Complaining, worrying.

Wimple: To wander.

Winna: Will not.

Winnock: Window.

Wud: Wild.

Wyte: Blame.

Yeld: Dried up.

Yestreen: Last night.

Yill: Ale.

Yin: One.

Yont: Beyond.

FOR FURTHER READING

G.W.S. Barrow, *The Kingdom of the Scots*.
David Bellingham, *An Introduction to Celtic Mythology*.
Raymond Buckland, *Scottish Witchcraft*.
Nora Chadwick, *The Celts*.
R.M. Douglas, *Scottish Lore and Folklore*.
A.A.M. Duncan, *Scotland: The Making of the Kingdom*.
Dorothy Hartley, *Lost Country Life*.
I. Henderson, *The Picts*.
Gerhard Herm, *The Celts*.
Proinsias Mac Cana, *Celtic Mythology*.
J.D. Mackie, *A History of Scotland*.
Charles MacKinnon, *Scottish Highlanders*.
R. Nicholson, *Scotland: The Later Middle Ages*.
N.J. O'Conor, *Battles and Enchantments, Retold from Early Gaelic Literature*.
D. Parry-Jones, *Welsh Legends and Fairy Lore*.
Nigel Pennick, *The Pagan Book of Days*.
Stuart Piggott, *The Druids*.
Alwyn and Brinley Rees, *Celtic Heritage*.

Sir John Rys, *Celtic Folklore, Welsh and Manx.*

Sir Walter Scot, *Manners, Customs, and History of the Highlanders of Scotland.*

Jacqueline Simpson, *The Folklore of Sussex.*

F.T. Wainwright, ed., *The Problems of the Picts.*

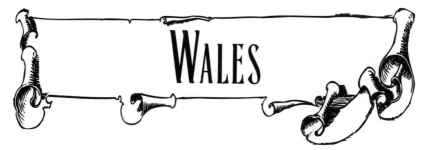

CHAPTER TWENTY-SIX

WALES

n the Dark Ages, raids by Englishmen led to the building of Offa's dyke (second half of the eighth century) which established a clear border between the two nations and prevented unwanted cattle theft and raids. Though broken in places, the earthen-work dyke ran from the Wye River to the Dee estuary. King Offa also built his dyke to more effectively control the trade of the area.

But the English weren't the only ones to plague the Welsh. Starting in the ninth century, the Vikings came to their shores. Throughout the next two hundred years, Wales was continually harassed by both the Vikings and the English (the English demanded they submit to the English kings).

Inner political conflicts also plagued the Welsh, especially in the mid-eleventh century when Gruffydd ap Rhydderch and Gruffydd ap Llywelyn vied for control. Both employed a number of English and Viking mercenaries. Ap Llywelyn's victory of 1055 over ap Rhydderch was short lived. In 1063, the English killed him and from that point on, the English claimed the right to name the Welsh king.

William the Conqueror also set his sights on Wales and not long after his invasion of England, he, too, sent troops. By 1093, England controlled the southern regions.

During the reign of King Stephen when English control was rocked by civil war, Wales reasserted itself. The princes furthered their control by signing pacts with Henry II, Simon de Montfort and Henry III. In the Treaty of Montgomery (1267), Llywelyn ap Gruffydd was named the Prince of Wales and was allowed to rule over most of the Welsh lands.

But in 1276, problems again arose. Llewelyn ap Gruffydd and Edward I came to blows that ended with Llewelyn confined to

Gwynedd. Llewelyn attempted once more to retake his former position in 1282, but only succeeded in bringing about his own death and establishing English control over Wales.

In 1284, Gwynedd was split into three shires: Anglesey, Caernarvon and Merioneth, all of which were under English control. Other shires were reorganized and the Flint shire area was created.

Edward began building castles on the borders to ensure his control. And in 1301, Edward I gave his son, Edward II, the title of Prince of Wales. Throughout the fourteenth century, Welsh uprisings and rebellions occurred, but still the English maintained their power.

During the fifteenth century, Owain Glyndwr managed to lead a strong rebellion. For the first time in more than one hundred years, a Welsh prince exercised the powers born to him. But his reign was short. Around 1410, his power failed and Wales was thrown into a period of anarchy until 1485 when Henry Tudor took the throne of England.

✤ ✤ ✤

VOCABULARY

Aberth: Sacrifice.

Abid: Apparel.

Abo: Prey.

Abwyd: Worm.

Achenog: Beggar.

Achlesu: Cherish.

Achlod: Disgrace.

Addien: Beautiful.

Adduned: Vow.

Aderyn: Bird.

Adwr: Coward.

Adwyth: Evil.

Aeth: Pain.

Aflan: Foul.

Agweddi: Dowry.

Aillt: Vassal.

Alarch: Swan.

Allfro: Foreigner.

Amherchi: Dishonor.

Angall: Foolish.

Anghenfil: Monster.

Angyles: Angel.

Arglwydd: Lord.

Baban: Baby.

Bachgen: Boy.

Bachgennes: Young girl.

Bachgennyn: Young boy.

Bachigyn: Little one.

Balchder: Pride.

Banon: Queen.

Baran: Rage.

Bardd: Poet.

Barwn: Baron.

Barwnes: Baroness.

Barwnig: Baronet.

Benyw: Woman.

Bidog: Dagger.

Biswail: Dung.

Boneddiges: Lady.

Brawd: Brother.

Brenin: King.

Briallen: Primrose.

Byw: Quick.

Cariad: Beloved.

Casau: Hate.

Ceffyl: Horse.

Chwaer: Sister.

Cleddyf: Sword.

Colomen: Dove.

Cwningen: Rabbit.

Cymen: Prim.

Cyndyn: Headstrong.

Cythraul: Devil.

Delfrydol: Ideal.

Distewi: Quiet.

Draig: Dragon.

Dyn: Man.

Eglwys: Church.

Erchyll: Horrible.

Gweddw: Widow.

Gwobr: Prize.

Gwr: Husband.

Gwraig: Wife.

Gwyry: Virgin.

Hardd: Handsome.

Hurtyn: Idiot.

Ie: Yes.

Ilachar: Radiant.

Llances: Young woman.

Maeden: Hussy.

Mam: Mother.

Meddwyn: Drunkard.

Meistr: Master.

Meistres: Mistress.

Monchyn: Pig.

Mor-forwyn: Siren.

Morwyn: Damsel.

Nef: Heaven.

Ni: No.

Offeiriad: Priest.

Prydferth: Handsome.

Putain: Harlot.

Rhyfelwr: Warrior.

Sarff: Snake.

Sarrug: Grim.

Sofliar: Quail.

Tad: Father.

Tawel: Quiet.

Tywysog: Prince.

FOR FURTHER READING

David Bellingham, *An Introduction to Celtic Mythology*.
Nora Chadwick, *The Celts*.
R.R. Davies, *Conquest, Coexistence and Change: Wales 1063 to 1415*.
———— *Lordship and Society in the March of Wales 1282 to 1400*.
W. Davies, *Wales in the Early Middle Ages*.
D. Fox, *Offa's Dyke*.
Jeffrey Gantz, *The Mabinogion*.

Gerald of Wales, *The Journey Through Wales/The Description of Wales*.

R. Griffiths, *The Principality of Wales in the Later Middle Ages*.

W.L. Griffiths, *The Welsh*.

Gerhard Herm, *The Celts*.

K.H. Jackson, *A Celtic Miscellany*.

J.E. Lloyd, *History of Wales from the Earliest Times to the Edwardian Conquest*.

Proinsias Mac Cana, *Celtic Mythology*.

D. Parry-Jones, *Welsh Legends and Fairy Lore*.

Stuart Piggott, *The Druids*.

Alwyn and Brinley Rees, *Celtic Heritage*.

William Rees, *South Wales and the March 1284 to 1415*.

A.J. Roderick, ed., *Wales Through the Ages*.

Sir John Rys, *Celtic Folklore, Welsh and Manx*.

D. Thomas, ed., *Wales: A New Study*.

David Walker, *Medieval Wales*.

————— *The Norman Conquerors*.

A.H. Williams, *An Introduction to the History of Wales* (2 vols).

G.A. Williams, *When Was Wales? A History of the Welsh*.

Glanmore Williams, *The Welsh Church from Conquest to Reformation*.

————— *History of Wales* (2 vols.).

CHAPTER TWENTY-SEVEN

IRELAND

reland was settled by the Celts between 600 and 150 B.C. They entered the land and set up petty kingdoms with a large number of kings, perhaps as many as one hundred at a time. Christianity came to the Celts during the fifth century A.D. when the first missionary, Bishop Palladius, arrived. The spread of Christianity was a slow one.

Over the next hundred years, the Celts formed a separate branch of Christianity that held until the Synod of Whitby in 662 where St. Columba agreed to submit the Celtic Church to their Roman counterpart.

During the Dark Ages, art actually flourished in Ireland. Marvelous manuscripts, jewelry and masonry were produced by monks and secular artists. Their distinctive circular scroll style is definitive even today. In addition to this, Ireland became an important seat for learning with its schools and teachers ranked as the best in Europe.

However, by the eighth century, most of the religiosity had passed and lay powers vied for control of the Irish churches and their property.

Due to their political structure of multiple kings who were elected from a royal dynasty and a lack of a feudal system, the Irish were an easy target for the Viking raiders of the eighth century. Though the kings did have lakeside strongholds called *crannogs*, they were still nothing more than tribal chieftains. The tuaths (kingdoms) were grouped into five overkingdoms: Ulster, Meath, Connacht, Munster and Leinster. However, no king was strong enough to rule anything more than his own kingdom.

The static power structure of the Celts proved a great handicap when dealing with the Danish threat. It wasn't until 1014 under the leadership of Brian Boru that the Celts began to turn back the Viking invaders. Finally, Ireland had her High King.

However, they were not so fortunate when the Anglo-Normans, under the direction of Henry II, showed up 150 years later. Though armed with a license from Pope Adrian IV instructing the English king to "root out the weeds of vice," Henry delayed his attack on Ireland from 1155 to 1171.

Yet for all Henry's intentions (the primary one not being the Holy one to reform the church, but to control the English who had already established lands there), he was unable to quell the whole of Ireland. Instead, Ireland ended up divided into three categories: the western coast which refused to submit to the invaders, the Pale (or Dublin and its surrounding areas) where the English had total control, and the areas beyond the Pale where the English lords built their own castles and controlled their demesne.

In 1175, High King Rory O'Connor granted Henry overlordship of Ireland with the Treaty of Windsor. This English claim was furthered in 1254 when Henry III granted Ireland to his son Edward.

As the English mingled and intermarried with the Irish, the English brought the Celtic Church more under the control and standards of the Roman. Throughout the thirteenth century, the English reformed the Irish political system and by the end of that century, an Irish parliament was introduced that mirrored its English counterpart.

But the Irish resisted English control, a rebellion that resulted in Robert the Bruce joining his brother in Ireland in 1317 to help fight the English. However, the war was far from over. In 1366 the Statutes of Kilkenny outlawed all Gaelic customs. Such bans furthered the gulf between the Anglo-Irish and the native Irish.

By the fifteenth century, things began to settle. Until 1495 when the Drogheda parliament bound Ireland firmly to English control and ended any independence of the Irish parliamentary.

FOR FURTHER READING

P.W. Asplin, *Medieval Ireland: A Bibliography of Secondary Works.*
J.C. Beckett, *A History of Ireland.*
Ludwig Bieler, *St. Patrick and the Coming of Christianity.*
Rachel Bromwich, *Medieval Celtic Literature: A Select Bibliography.*

F.J. Byrne, *Irish Kings and High Kings*.
Edmund Curtis, *A History of Medieval Ireland*.
Maire and Liam de Paor, *Early Christian Ireland*.
Liam de Paor, *The Peoples of Ireland*.
Peter Harbison, *The Archaeology of Ireland*.
Kathleen Hughes, *The Church in Early Irish Society*.
————— *Early Christian Ireland*.
J.F. Lydon, *The Lordship of Ireland in the Middle Ages*.
————— *Ireland in the Later Middle Ages*.
Seumas MacManus, *The Story of the Irish Race*.
J.T. MacNeill, *The Celtic Churches: A History A.D. 200 to 1200*.
Donnchadh O. Corrain, *Ireland Before the Normans*.
G.H. Orpen, *Ireland Under the Normans (4 vols.)*.
A.J. Otway-Ruthven, *A History of Medieval Ireland*.
John Ranelagh, *Ireland: An Illustrated History*.

APPENDIX

GENERAL REFERENCE TEXTS

F.B. Andrews, *The Medieval Builder and His Methods*.

Philippe Aries and Georges Duby, eds., *A History of Private Life: Revelations of the Medieval World*.

J.W. Baldwin, *The Scholastic Culture of the Middle Ages 1000 to 1300*.

Richard Barber, *The Penguin Guide to Medieval Europe*.

Frank Barlow, *The Feudal Kingdom of England 1042 to 1216*.

Morris Bishop, *The Middle Ages*.

Marc Bloch, *Feudal Society* (2 vols).

John Boswell, *Christianity, Social Tolerance and Homosexuality*.

Ruth Brantl, ed., *Medieval Culture: The Image and the City*.

Asa Briggs, ed., *Reader's Digest Everyday Life Through the Ages*.

Christopher Brooke, *Europe in the Central Middle Ages 962 to 1154*.

Z.N. Brooke and C.W. Previte-Orton, eds., *The Cambridge Medieval History*, 8 vols.

James Burke, *Connections*.

————— *The Day the Universe Changed*.

N.F. Cantor, *The Civilization of the Middle Ages*.

————— *Inventing the Middle Ages*.

Andreas Capellanus, *The Art of Courtly Love*.

G.C. Coulton, *The Medieval Village*.

John Cummins, *The Hound and the Hawk: The Art of Medieval Hunting*.

R.H.C. Davis, *A History of Medieval Europe*.

————— *The Medieval Warhorse*.

D.C. Douglas, ed., *English Historical Documents* (12 vols).

Georges Duby, *The Chivalrous Society*.

————— *William Marshal: The Flower of Chivalry*.

F.L. Ganshof, *Feudalism*.

Frances and Joseph Gies, *Life in a Medieval Village*.

————— *Cathedral, Forge, and Waterwheel: Technology and Invention in the Middle Ages*.

Felix Grendon, *Anglo-Saxon Charms*.

Hammond Historical Atlas of the World.

Elizabeth Hallam, *The Plantagenet Encyclopedia*.

————— *The Plantagenet Chronicles*.

B.A. Hanawalt, *The Ties that Bound: Peasant Families in Medieval Europe*.

————— *Crime and Conflict in English Communities 1300 to 1348*.

Denys Hay, *Europe in the Fourteenth and Fifteenth Centuries*.

————— *The Medieval Centuries*.

Rodney Hilton, *Bond Men Made Free: Medieval Peasant Movements and the English Rising of 1381.*

U.T. Holmes, Jr., *Daily Living in the Twelfth Century.*

V.F. Hopper and G.B. Lahey, eds., *Medieval Mysteries, Moralities, and Interludes.*

Friedrich Heer, *The Medieval World.*

David Herlihy, ed., *Medieval Culture and Society.*

J.C. Holt, *Magna Carta.*

Johan Huizinga, *Men and Ideas: History, the Middle Ages, the Renaissance.*

Maurice Keen, *Medieval Europe.*

————— *Outlaws of Medieval Legend.*

Sherrilyn Kenyon, *Writer's Digest Character Naming Sourcebook.*

Jacques le Goff, *Intellectuals in the Middle Ages.*

H.R. Loyn, ed., *The Middle Ages: a Concise Encyclopedia.*

F.W. Maitland, *Domesday Book and Beyond.*

Andrew McCall, *The Medieval Underworld.*

Colin McEvedy, *The Penguin Atlas of Medieval History.*

Michel Mollat, *The Poor in the Middle Ages.*

Catherine Moriarty, ed., *The Voice of the Middle Ages: in Personal Letters 1100-1500.*

C.W.R.D. Moseley, trans., *The Travels of Sir John Mandeville.*

J.H. Mundy, *Europe in the High Middle Ages 1150 to 1309.*

A.R. Myers, *England in the Late Middle Ages 1307 to 1536.*

A.P. Newton, *Travel and Travellers in the Middle Ages.*

Tim Newark, *Medieval Warlords.*

Thomas F.X. Noble, *Europe from the Fifth Century to the Tenth.*

Sidney Painter, *William Marshal: Knight-Errant, Baron and Regent of England.*

Colin Platt, *The English Medieval Town.*

Eileen Power, *Medieval People.*

F.M. Powicke, *Ways of Medieval Life and Thought.*

J.R. Reinhard, *Medieval Pageant.*

J.B. Ross and M.M. McLaughlin, *The Portable Medieval Reader.*

Trevor Rowley, *The High Middle Ages 1200 to 1550.*

————— *The Norman Heritage 1066 to 1200.*

Joseph Strayer, ed., *Dictionary of the Middle Ages*, 13 vols.

————— *On the Medieval Origins of the Modern State.*

Barbara Swain, *Fools and Folly during the Middle Ages and the Renaissance.*

Brian Tierney, *The Middle Ages Vol. I: Sources of Medieval History*.
————— *The Middle Ages Vol. II: Readings in Medieval History*.
B. Wilkinson, *The Later Middle Ages in England*.
Zolar's Encyclopedia of Omens, Signs, and Superstitions.

INDEX